FORAGE IN SPRING

THE FOOD AND MEDICINE OF BRITAIN'S WILD PLANTS

ROBIN HARFORD

Copyright © 2022 by Robin Harford

Robin Harford has asserted his rights as author of this work in accordance with the Copyright, Designs and Patents Act 1988.

All rights reserved. No part of this publication may be reproduced, stored in a retrieval system, or transmitted, in any form, by any means, electronic, mechanical, photocopying, recording or otherwise, without written permission of the publisher unless in accordance with the provisions of the Copyright Designs and Patents Act 1988.

Great care has been taken to maintain the accuracy of the information contained in this work. However, neither the publisher, the editor nor author can be held responsible for any consequences arising from use of the information contained herein. The views expressed in this work are those of the author and do not necessarily reflect those of the publisher.

ISBN: 978-1-915823-01-4

Second edition published in 2022 by

Eatweeds Press, Exeter, Devon, UK

www.eatweeds.co.uk

For my beautiful Family

CONTENTS

Introduction — vii
Safety and sustainability guidelines — ix

1. Alexanders — 1
2. Brooklime — 14
3. Cleavers (Goosegrass) — 24
4. Dandelion — 36
5. Garlic Mustard — 48
6. Ground Elder — 58
7. Ground Ivy — 70
8. Plantain — 80
9. Primrose — 100
10. Ramsons (Wild Garlic) — 112
11. Sea Beet — 126
12. Smooth Sowthistle — 138
13. Sorrel — 154
14. Stinging Nettle — 170
15. Sweet Violet — 196

Continue The Journey — 209
About the Author — 211
Bibliography — 213

INTRODUCTION

It is my intention to help you become a plant ambassador. Someone who loves their local flora enough to want to protect it and be a voice for the plants.

My plant mentor Frank Cook always said:

> If you know one plant really well, then teach it to others.

This is how we spread our love of plants. It isn't about becoming an expert or a teacher per se, it is about changing the culture, one plant at a time.

Our plant heritage is slowly being forgotten and it is people like you who can change that.

Start sharing what you learn within the pages of this book with others.

Create wild food meals and ask your friends and loved ones over. Take them out plant spotting. Bring the wildness of the world into your home. Surround yourself with green.

See this as a journey down the Green Path. An exciting adventure. Become a playful plant explorer. Enjoy the ride. It's going to be a blast.

I hope some day our paths will cross, until then, happy gathering.

SAFETY AND SUSTAINABILITY GUIDELINES

Foraging is all about sustainability.

The relationship between plants and people.

How we engage with the natural world without violating it.

Humans are grazing animals and have as much right to be in the ecosystem as any other animal.

The hysterical newspaper headlines and armchair conservationists shout that foragers are evil pillagers who destroy habitats and biodiversity.

> According to the UK State of Nature report, issued in September 2019 by a grouping of over seventy nature conservation organisations, the major pressures on the UK's nature are: unsustainable forms of agricultural and woodland management, climate change, urbanisation, pollution, hydrological change and invasive non-native species.
>
> — BIODIVERSITY IN THE UK: BLOOM OR BUST? A HOUSE OF COMMONS COMMITTEE REPORT

Foragers are some of the most ecologically aware people around and are deeply embedded with their environment.

You don't destroy what you love, care and have respect for.

SUSTAINABLE HARVESTING GUIDELINES

Here is my advice so you can become a responsible, safe and sustainable forager.

- Try and harvest away from other humans. Some people think picking any wildflower is illegal. It isn't. This minimises the possibility for potential confrontation. See https://www.eatweeds.co.uk/foraging-and-the-law

- Only gather what you will use today and maybe tomorrow. One in ten (10%) is the best ratio to go by. This leaves most of the plant stand (community) for other non-humans and has a minimal impact on the ecosystem.

If you go over this you are gathering from plant communities that are too small.

Every plant is different in how much harvesting it can tolerate. Some thrive when harvested heavily. Others will be impacted and might decline.

Foraging requires paying close attention to how your harvesting protocols impact your local land-base. Each plant and ecosystem is unique.

- Only harvest perennials. Picking them does not usually threaten their survival.

- Never harvest endangered, rare or threatened species.

A plant might be recorded as scarce or rare in one county yet grow in abundance in another. Know the local status of a plant.

- Contact a local botany group and go through your list of plants with someone there. See https://bsbi.org/local-botany

- Learn the flora in your county. Approach this as a journey, an exciting game. Become a plant explorer. See https://bsbi.org/county-floras

THE GOLDEN RULES

- Never eat any plant you do not have a 100% positive identification for. This means you are absolutely certain you have the correct plant.

- If you catch yourself thinking - "I think it is" - you do not know.

- If in doubt, leave it out. Never munch on a hunch.

LEARN TO FORAGE SAFELY

If you'd like to deepen your foraging skills, why not come on one of my foraging courses. Details can be found at:

https://www.eatweeds.co.uk/foraging-courses

WHAT THE PRESS ARE SAYING

'Highly rated' - The Guardian

'A revelation!' - BBC Good Food Magazine

'One of Britain's most dedicated foragers' - The Lady

1
ALEXANDERS

A native of Mediterranean Europe and naturalised in Britain since the days of the Romans, Alexanders (*Smyrnium olusatrum*) was the parsley of Alexandria, or *petroselinum Alexandrinum* in medieval Latin. There is some evidence that the Romans brought the plant to Britain to use as a culinary and medicinal herb because of its aromatic parts. This forgotten herb, once popular in ancient kitchen gardens, now thrives in abundance by the sea. It was cultivated for centuries as a common table vegetable across Europe until it was eventually replaced by the milder-tasting celery.

Like many Umbellifer plants, Alexanders exudes aromatic oils with a pungent, sweet smell that attracts a wide range of pollinating insects. According to Roman physician Pliny (70 AD) it gained the name '*Smyrnium*' because of the distinctive myrrh-like fragrance of the fruits; the thickened tap root is also fragrant.

FOOD

"It is one of my favourite wild foods," wrote Peter Wyse Jackson, "although some people tell me they find it revolting." He added: "The delicate flavour is somewhat reminiscent of fennel or celery. March is the ideal month to collect and use it. Later in the season the shoots become woody and stringy, and the flavour becomes too strong for my taste."

The coast is littered with Alexanders where it was once gathered as a wild vegetable and potherb. As well as in coastal areas, Alexanders is commonly found on monastic sites or among castle ruins, where the wild edible was once cultivated by monks and is a relic of ancient kitchen gardens. Archaeological research at a medieval market site in Rotterdam, the Netherlands, has uncovered evidence that Alexanders was once used as a kitchen herb, and its use is also referred to in early medieval sources such as the Carolingian text *Capitulare de villis vel curtis imperii* (written around 812 AD), which recommends seventy-three medicinal plants to be cultivated on Charlemagne's royal estate.

Some authorities suggest Alexanders was introduced to the British Isles by the Romans, who used it as a vegetable and medicinal herb. Caprioli and team tell us it was a popular wild edible during the time of Alexander the Great in the fourth century BC. Dioscorides also knew Alexanders as a vegetable and condiment, and Greek naturalist Theophrastus (371–287 BC) described it as a delicious plant.

Alexanders fell out of use from the seventeenth century but had by that time established itself as a wild plant, or weed, growing among cultivated crops.

It was once known as 'black potherb' because its ripened seeds are black, and bring a sharp, spicy aroma to any dish. *Herbalpedia* tells us: "It is from the black 'twin' seed that the plant takes its name of black pot herb, the seed being used to flavor stews." The species name can be broken down into *Olus*, meaning 'potherb', and *atrum*, meaning 'black', because the ripened fruit are very black in colour. Before the advent of celery, this 'black potherb' had many culinary uses as described by English herbalist John Parkinson (1567–1650):

> "The tops of the rootes, with the lower part of the stalkes of Alisanders, are used in Lent especially, and Spring of the yeare, to make broth, which although it be a little bitter, yet it is both wholesome, and pleasing to a great many, by reason of the aromaticall or spicie taste, warming and comforting the stomack, and helping it digest the many waterish and flegmaticke meates [which] are in those times much eaten. The rootes also either rawe or boyled are often eaten with oyle and vinegar."

The reasoning behind the herb's use at Lent may be that it was thought to have 'purging' qualities. A soup made of Alexanders, watercress and nettles was called 'Lenten pottage' by Irish matrons, as recorded in Scully's *Flora of Co. Kerry* (1916).

Like Parkinson, English botanist and herbalist John Gerard (1545–1612) also recommended that the leaves and stalks boiled could be eaten alone or dressed. He suggested they were preferable pickled and that the root could be eaten raw, which was good for the stomach.

As a medieval potherb, Alexanders was popular for soups and stews. English gardener and diarist John Evelyn (1620–1706) suggested in his gardening notes that Alexanders be included among the "plants of the Kitchen-Garden". He praised it further in his *Acetaria: A Discourse of Sallets* (1699) as a "moderately hot" herb that is cleansing, nourishing and comforting to the stomach.

> "The gentle fresh Sprouts, Buds, and Tops are to be chosen, and the Stalks eaten in the Spring; and when Blanch'd, in Winter likewise, with Oyl, Pepper, Salt, &c. by themselves, or in Composition: They make also an excellent Vernal [spring] Pottage."

Alexanders was grown in Elizabethan gardens in Britain as an aromatic addition to fish and seafood dishes. The herb was also introduced to North America by colonists in the sixteenth century. As a common garden vegetable its characteristic flavour was a welcome addition to home-made recipes. However, its pungency may have equally contributed to its downfall. Caprioli and team wrote:

> "Its marginalization has to be related to direct competition with the improved form of celery (*Apium graveolens* L.) as a consequence of the changing tastes in the Western world, i.e. from dishes rich in spices and bitter and/or pungent ingredients towards milder dishes with respect to the flavour of the food itself."

Richard Mabey (1978) suggested that the plant's "cloying angelica smell" is reduced in cooking.

It seems a shame that this truly fascinating plant with a lot of potential is rarely picked for culinary use in today's kitchens. Its flavour, though similar to celery, is unique, and it can be blanched like celery, steamed like spinach or served up like asparagus, dressed with butter. Nutritionally, recent studies have found that Alexanders' fruits are a rich source of protein and carbohydrates, which makes the plant worthy of addition to hearty meals and healthy salads. The fruits are also a good source of fatty acids, which help to reduce incidences of chronic disease, such as heart disease. Research by Maggi and team found that Alexanders has an abundance of plant sugars and bioactive compounds, such as flavonoids, which makes it a wild edible truly worthy of rediscovery:

> "The levels of ascorbic acid detected and the nutritional profile exhibited partially supported the traditional use of Alexanders as an antiscorbutic remedy and suggest its re-acceptance as a vegetable would be worthwhile."

An earlier paper by the same authors emphasised the versatility of the herb:

> "The fruits are used to flavour meat, soups and salads, and as a substitute for pepper; the raw or cooked roots are served at table, often as a substitute for parsnips".

Jackson suggested collecting the young shoots or stalks early in the season, just as the plant is beginning to flower, because it can become tough and stringy later in the year. "March is the ideal month to collect and use it." The young shoots and stalks are particularly flavoursome and provide a versatile spring vegetable that can be cut, boiled and served with butter or added to soups, broths, stews, meat casseroles and fish dishes for flavouring.

Leaves and flowers can also be added to soups, or alternatively the delicate leaves and flowerheads make spicy additions to salads. The leaves, or any leftover pieces of the plant that have been prepared for cooking, can be shredded to make coleslaw. The flower buds can be pickled, fried into fritters or steamed in place of broccoli. The thicker stems can also be blanched and eaten as a vegetable. The flower stem is the most succulent part of the plant, although it needs peeling and can be eaten raw or cooked. I prefer them lightly steamed and dressed with lashings of butter.

Alexanders' roots can bring seasonal variety to Sunday roasts when cooked and eaten like parsnips, to which they taste similar. They can even be candied in sugar like angelica. Keep the roots tender by storing in a cool place in winter. Grind the ripe seeds like pepper for an authentic seasoning to flavour meat, salads and hot dishes. In a letter to *The Times* on 7 May 1988, from a writer in East Sussex, Alexanders leaves were recommended as a herb for white sauce, and the braised stems as an alternative to asparagus. Several other sources suggest the plant's leaves are a good choice of flavouring for white sauce. The leafy seedlings can also be used as a parsley substitute.

The weedy plant has caught the attention of celebrity chefs. Hugh Fearnley-Whittingstall, the British TV chef, recently revealed a recipe for Alexanders liqueur on *A River Cottage Christmas*. The shoots and leaves were liquidised and the juice boiled and added to sugar. A few parts vodka helped to make the liqueur.

Thus there are many culinary uses for this forgotten herb: in soups, stews, casseroles, fish and meat dishes; in salads; as a side vegetable dressed in butter; or as candied roots and stems. The wild edible was once popular in Italy as a vegetable and it's still added to fish dishes in some regions such as Abruzzi and Apulia. For example, in Sicily, Alexanders is added to aromatic soups made with pulses, and used to accompany fish dishes and to spice up salads with cheese. In Sardinia, Turkey and Spain, the leaves are eaten as greens. In Aegean regions, the leaf stalks are eaten raw, cooked or added to pickles.

In coastal regions of Britain, local people pick the wild edible where it grows prolifically by the sea. The plant was also cultivated in Syria and in the Canary Islands.

If the distinctive flavour of *S. olusatrum* doesn't win you over, perhaps the taste of *S. perfoliatum* (perfoliate Alexanders) might.

Facciola commented that this herb is considered superior to Alexanders because it is "crisp and tender, and not so harsh flavored".

Alternatively, you don't need to cook the herb to benefit from its myrrh-like scent; simply add the dried seeds to potpourri. In past times, the stalks of Alexanders were bundled and used as fuel. The plant has also been used as cattle fodder.

RECIPES

Buttered Alexanders

- 3 handfuls of chopped alexanders stems (leaves removed)
- 2 large knobs of butter & a glug of olive oil
- 1 lime (juiced)
- sea salt & cracked black pepper

Gently boil the chopped alexanders for 2 minutes in water, then drain. Melt the butter with the olive oil and gently fry the alexanders on low for a good 15 minutes. Fry them until they are very, very soft. The slower and softer you can cook them the better they will taste. Towards the end add the juiced lime, and put a lid on the pan. Steam fry on medium in the lime juice for about 30 seconds. Serve with crushed sea salt to taste. If you leave them overnight in the fridge, they turn into a thick buttery dish once warmed back up to room temperature, and the flavours have had time to meld. Serves 3

Alexanders Chutney

- 500g Alexanders stems (chopped)
- 3 x onions (chopped)
- 200g sugar

- ¼ cup sherry vinegar
- ¼ cup red wine vinegar
- 1½ tsp mustard powder
- ½ tsp turmeric powder
- 1 tbsp cornflour
- 35ml of water

Boil Alexanders stems and onions in just enough salted water to cover, cook until al dente then strain. Put back in the pan with the sugar and vinegar, and boil for 15 minutes. Meanwhile mix the mustard, turmeric, cornflour and eighth pint of water into a smooth paste, then stir into the Alexanders and boil for 15 minutes or longer if the mixture needs thickening more. Sterilise the jars, then fill with chutney and cap.

Pickled Buds of Alexanders

- 500ml of Alexanders buds
- 25g of salt
- 25g of fresh ginger
- 300ml of white wine vinegar

Collect 500ml of Alexanders buds, and blanch them for 10 seconds in boiling water to which you have added the salt. Strain off and allow to cool. Peel and thinly slice the fresh ginger. Fill a sterilised jar with the Alexanders buds and sliced ginger. Now pour over cold vinegar and seal. You can start eating this recipe after three days.

MEDICINE

When sailors went ashore, they picked Alexanders up and down the coast as a 'healthy herb'. Gabrielle Hatfield (2007) tells us: "Quelch in *Herbs for Daily Use* (1941) reported that 'stories were told of crews being allowed to go ashore at Anglesea that they might gather and cook the herb'." It was an old seafaring remedy for scurvy, particularly when other sources of vitamin C were not as readily available, and for cleansing blood. It was also used in this way in Scotland. In the coastal county of Dorset, England, the weed was called 'helrut', possibly derived from 'health-root' or a corruption of 'heal root'.

Alexanders was valued for its warming and curative actions by English botanist, herbalist and physician Nicholas Culpeper (1616–1654). Culpeper echoed the words of Gerard when he wrote that the plant could be prescribed to: "move women's courses [referring to menstruation], to expel the afterbirth, to break wind, to provoke urine, and help the stranguary [painful urination]". An all-round helpful herb for the gastro-urinary and female reproductive systems, it seemed. John Pechey (1655–1716) also recommended Alexanders for strengthening the stomach and cleansing blood. Moncrief's *Poor Man's Physician* (in the eighteenth century) recommended the seeds for febrile convulsions, while other herbalists recommended the seeds for flatulence or as a stimulant.

Around the time of these great English herbalists, Alexanders was sold as 'horse parsley' at Covent Garden Market in London, England. The roots were considered a cure for 'gravel', or small urinary stones.

The ancient Greeks and Romans also valued Alexanders as a digestive herb. The fruits were taken to relieve stomach problems; the juice of the root was considered to be both diuretic (increasing urination) and laxative, as well as an appetite stimulant; the leaves could be used to prevent or treat scurvy. In Libyan folk medicine, Alexanders was considered to be calefacient – a warming herb – and used in a decoction to cure chest colds or headaches. The fruits were ground to powder and mixed with water. Greek physician

Dioscorides (40–90 AD) recommended the herb for dropsy – an ancient term for the swelling of soft tissues in the body – probably for its diuretic effects. A fifteenth-century leechdom, or remedy, also recommends Alexanders "for all manner of dropsies". It goes on to say:

> "Take sage and betony, crop and root, even portions, and seed of Alexanders, and seed of sow thistle, and make them into a powder, of each equally much; and powder half an ounce of spikenard of Spain, put it thereto, and then put all these together in a cake of white dough and put it in a stewpan full of good ale, and stop it well; and give it the sick to drink all day."

In the Scottish Hebrides of the eighteenth century, a nourishing lamb broth made with lovage and Alexanders was eaten to help the body fight the wasting disease consumption, now known as tuberculosis. In the Isle of Man, where the plant was known as 'lus-ny-ollee', Alexanders was used to treat toothache in humans and mouth sores in cattle scurvy. The crushed leaves or juice were used to heal minor cuts and bruises. The plant was also a remedy for asthma.

To briefly recap on the historical medicinal use of Alexanders, it has been used since antiquity as a bitter herb to provoke urination, stimulate digestion or cure dropsy. The seeds were a treatment for scurvy (we now know that they contain vitamin C) and to promote menstruation. The crushed leaves or their juice were used to heal cuts and bruises, or as a treatment for asthma.

Hatfield wrote that Alexanders fell out of favour from the mid-nineteenth century onwards and is little used by today's herbalists. "Now it grows in unharvested abundance along field edges and beside ruins, its presence a dim reminder of the sites of earlier monastic kitchen gardens."

It is still used in some parts of the Mediterranean as a medicine-food, such as in Cyprus where it is eaten for its antiseptic, digestive and tonic properties.

The whole plant yields essential oils which contain furanosesquiterpenoids – a class of compound responsible for the odour of myrrh and turmeric. Maggi and team have shown that Alexanders has a biologically active component called isofuranodiene, which may have anticancer effects. In laboratory tests, isofuranodiene inhibited the growth of colon cancer cells and of uterine and breast cancer cells, even enhancing the effectiveness of chemotherapy treatments such as tamoxifen. The authors concluded that the plant may be of further interest to the pharmaceutical industry for its active constituents and for its easy cultivation as a flavouring for food.

Research by Quassinti and team in 2014 found that isofuranodiene in Alexanders inhibits growth in colon cancer cells. The aim of the study was to provide an evidence base for the "recovery of wild celery [Alexanders] as a widely-used vegetable as well as a potential source to be exploited for the development of chemopreventive agents".

In the same year, Caprioli and team investigated the ascorbic acid content of Alexanders to understand its traditional use as a remedy for scurvy. The authors concluded that while some parts of the plant did contain vitamin C, its content was comparable to that found in cultivated celery and lower than in other well-known sources of vitamin C, such as oranges and kiwi.

SAFETY NOTE

The herb *S. olusatrum* has been recorded as abortive in some texts. Other than this, there are few contraindications documented about its use. As Alexanders is seldom used in food and medicine, it's possible that little data exists about its potential toxicity. Nevertheless, exercise caution in pregnancy and when breastfeeding.

BOTANICAL PROFILE

Scientific Name: *Smyrnium olusatrum.*

Family: Apiaceae.

Botanical Description

Height: up to 1.5 m. Flowers: greenish-yellow flowers in umbrella-like clusters carry a pungent, myrrh-like scent. Leaves: glossy, bright-green leaves, toothed and formed in groups of three at the end of the leaf stalk; similar in appearance to celery. Fruit: two globular halves form a fruit with prominent ridges. Ripen to a black colour. Foliage: leaves and flowers are similar to wild angelica, for which the plant is sometimes mistaken. Root: thick, black roots with white flesh.

Flowers: April to June.

Status: Biennial. Mediterranean native.

Habitat: Sea cliffs, hedgerows, roadsides, wasteland.

Alexanders (*Smyrnium olusatrum*)

2
BROOKLIME

Brooklime (*Veronica beccabunga*) is a delicate blue flower of ponds and streams, and often grows with watercress. It was used for centuries as a salad plant in northern Europe, collected in spring and well known for its pungency and bitterness.

Indeed, its species name *'beccabunga'* means 'pungent'. Maude Grieve suggested in *A Modern Herbal* (1931) that it derives from the Flemish *'beckpunge'*, meaning 'mouth smart'. She also referred to the plant's German name *'Bachbunge'*, with 'Bach' meaning 'brook' and *bunge* meaning 'bunch'.

The 'lime' in its common name is thought derived from an Anglo-Saxon word for the mud in which it grows.

FOOD

The bitter-tasting Brooklime is a wild edible that can be eaten like watercress – added raw to salads, or cooked like a potherb by boiling or steaming. The plant has been used in this way in northern Europe since the earliest times. Its flavour has been described as 'not unpleasant' by today's herbalists and foragers. Mrs Grieve wrote: "As a green vegetable, Brooklime is … wholesome, but not very palatable."

Brooklime is best mixed with other strongly flavoured greens to both compensate for and complement its bitterness. It is still appreciated as a bitter herb in Europe and Japan. The parts of the plant eaten include the young shoots, leaves and stems. In parts of Europe – the Czech Republic, Balkans, Bosnia and in the Basque regions – Brooklime is eaten as a raw salad leaf and cooked as a spring green. In the Czech Republic, the herb is an ingredient in some spirits.

Nutritionally, the Brooklime also contains 3.8 g of protein per 100 g of fresh weight (Kuhnlein and Turner, 1991). Several sources suggest the plant is rich in vitamin C. It also contains antioxidants, such as flavonoids and phenolics, which are reported to be a vital part of our diets in helping to reduce incidence of chronic disease.

The plant can be brewed as a tea, called *'tea de l'europe'* (or European tea), which has a flavour similar to Chinese green tea.

Note: When making recipes, only use very young shoots. The plant develops quite an intense bitterness, which some people like, the older it gets.

RECIPES

Brooklime Streamside

- 3 shallots – thinly sliced
- Butter
- 1-2 handfuls young brooklime shoots

- 1 tbsp honey
- 50ml vegetable stock
- Salt and pepper

Fry the shallots in butter until translucent and soft. Add the Brooklime shoots, vegetable stock, salt and pepper. Bring to the boil then reduce the heat and simmer until tender. Then add the honey.

Brooklime Asian Spring Soup

- 1 cup of Thai jasmine rice (sticky rice)
- 4 cups of water
- 3tbsp Thai tom-yum paste
- 1 six inch strip of dried kelp (cut into small strips)
- 2 cloves of garlic (chopped)
- 2 handfuls of young brooklime leaves and shoots

Put rice, tom-yum paste, kelp and water into a pan and bring to a simmering boil. Cook for 10 minutes (Jasmine rice usually only needs this long). Add garlic and Brooklime and simmer for a further 5 minutes. Stir often as the rice can start to stick to the bottom of the pan. Turn off heat, allow to cool, then serve in bowls.

Brooklime and Asparagus Side Dish

- 2 handfuls of very young Brooklime shoots
- 100g fine Asparagus
- Olive oil
- Cider vinegar
- Honey
- Cracked black pepper

Steam the Asparagus and towards the end of its cooking time, steam the Brooklime shoots for about 60 seconds. Allow to cool.

Combine the olive oil, cider vinegar and honey into a dressing and pour over the vegetables, serve with a sprinkling of cracked black pepper.

MEDICINE

In past times, Brooklime was much used medicinally as a "Diet Drink in the Spring against the Scurvy; it cleanseth the Kidneys of Gravel, and slimy Humours" (Threlkeld and Molyneux, 1727). It was a popular 'Spring Juice' for clearing out impurities and appeared in many seventeenth-century herbals and recipes as a cure for scurvy. The herb was recommended by the likes of John Gerard, Nicholas Culpeper and John Pechey. Before citrus fruits were imported, Brooklime was sold in London for sailors to take to sea to prevent scurvy. The plant's use as a treatment for scurvy continued in the nineteenth century, and it was mentioned in twentieth-century herbals as a diuretic and blood purifier. The juice was considered a purgative. Gerard (1597) said: "Brooke-lime is eaten in sallads as Water-Cresses are... The leaves of Brook-lime, and the tendrels of *Asparagus*, eaten with oyle, vineger, and Pepper, helpeth the strangurie and stone." Strangurie was a urinary tract infection.

Pechey (1707) gives a recipe for a scurvy remedy involving Brooklime:

"Take of the juice of Brooklime, Water-cresses and Scurvy-grass, each half a Pint; of the Juice of Oranges, four Ounces; fine Sugar, two Pounds; make a Syrup over a gentle Fire: Take one Spoonful in your Beer every time you drink".

Culpeper (1653) wrote about the plant:

"It is a hot and biting martial plant: Brooklime and water-cresses are generally used together in diet-drinks, with other things serving to purge the blood and body from ill-humours that would destroy health, and are helpful for the scurvy: they do also provoke urine, and help to break the stone, and pass it away; they provoke women's courses, and expel the dead child. Being fried with butter and vinegar, and applied warm, it helpeth all manner of tumours, swellings, and inflammations."

In Irish folk medicine, the plant was used "knotted … as a poultice to ease labour pains" (Uí Chonchubhair, 1995). It was also a traditional Irish remedy for coughs and colds, and again for for kidney and urinary complaints. Donald Watts (2007) wrote: "In Wicklow, too, the water in which it had been boiled was taken to be an excellent cold cure. One should stay in bed, however, as 'it opens all the pores'". The wild herb's use as a remedy for kidney and bladder complaints was probably due to its diuretic (increased urination) effects. In the fourteenth century Brooklime was also used to treat swellings, gout, tumours, liver problems and many other complaints.

An interesting story about an eighteenth-century Irish herbalist, Elizabeth Pearson, tells how she made a fortune by prescribing Brooklime for tuberculosis (then known as scrofula). Gabrielle Hatfield (2007) wrote:

"She was known as 'The Big Mrs Pearson' … It was her father-in-law who first aroused her interest in herbal matters, and she learned much from a gypsy whom she befriended. Soon she was brewing up the potion for which she became famous. This was apparently prepared behind locked doors in a stillroom."

By all accounts, Pearson's remedy was a huge success – perhaps too successful. In 1815, she petitioned parliament to officially recognise her cure, because she feared being tried as a witch.

Her famous recipe was preserved by her family as 'Pearson's Celebrated Cure for Scrofula':

"Take two large handfuls of Brooklime, cutting off the roots. Pound it as fine as you can, pour it into an old iron saucepan, with a pint of grounds of beer, a piece of salt butter, the size of a walnut, and as much rust of iron as would cover a penny. Let all boil, till the leaves sink to the bottom, then thicken with bran or oatmeal, until it is quite the right consistency for a poultice" (quoted in Hatfield, 2007).

As an age-old treatment for burns and wounds, Brooklime leaves were applied to injuries, and sometimes bruised to apply to ulcers and burns. In Britain, the plant was mentioned for treating 'bad legs', which may have referred to leg ulcers caused by scurvy. Gerard recommended the boiled herb for swollen legs and 'dropsy' (swollen body tissues).

Brooklime was well known for treating skin diseases. In the Balkans, a poultice of Brooklime, onions, wheat chaff and sour milk was made to treat skin complaints. Gypsies used the leaves as a poultice to cure piles and boils.

The wild edible was also used as a folk medicine to treat horses. In the seventeeth century, John Parkinson wrote: "Farryers do much use it about their horses to take away swellings, to heal the scab, and other like diseases in them".

It is not much employed by today's herbalists, according to Hatfield. A decoction of the leaves is sometimes recommended as a diuretic drink and to improve appetites. Guarrera and Savo (2016) states that Veronica beccabunga is known to have diuretic and appetizer properties.

Today we know that the plant contains vitamin C, as well as a glucoside (aucubine), and various other substances, such as sulphur.

James Duke added in his *Handbook of Medicinal Herbs* (2002) that Brooklime is an emmenagogue (promotes menstruation), and may be used to regulate irregular menstrual cycles. He also listed its use for anorexia, kidney and bladder complaints, water retention and swellings, fever, and for certain types of cancer. In Nepalese herbal medicine, the juice of the plant is also taken for fever. However, do ask your doctor for advice before using a herbal medicine to treat a serious medical condition.

As a cosmetic, Brooklime can be drunk as an infusion to keep skin clear and banish blemishes, or used externally as a face wash.

SAFETY NOTE

Mears and Hillman (2007) have raised concerns about eating Brooklime raw or lightly cooked, because it grows in nitrogen-rich habitats where liver fluke – a parasite that affects the liver – is present.

Duke wrote that there are few known side effects of taking Brooklime, although this is not proof of its safety. Do exercise caution when taking herbal remedies during pregnancy and breastfeeding, or in combination with prescribed medications.

BOTANICAL PROFILE

Scientific Name: *Veronica beccabunga.*

Family: Plantaginaceae.

Botanical Description

Flowers: tiny dark blue flowers; occasionally a pink form is found. The petals open wide in the sun and partially in shade. Fruit: a flat, round capsule containing winged seeds. Leaves: stalked, oval, glossy-green leaves that are leathery to the touch. Stems: succulent, hollow stems that creep in mud and root at the nodes.

Flowers: May to September.

Status: Perennial. Native.

Habitat: Ditches, meadow, ponds & pond edges, river banks.

Brooklime (*Veronica beccabunga*)

3
CLEAVERS (GOOSEGRASS)

Cleavers got its name from its ability to cling to clothing and fur, enabling it to hitch a lift from unsuspecting humans or animals. It's as familiar as burdock to pet owners who have spent hours disentangling cats and dogs from both bristly plants. As a common weed, it was known by many local names. Grieve (1931) wrote:

> "Its frequent name, Goosegrass, is a reference to the fact that geese are extremely fond of the herb. It is often collected for the purpose of giving it to poultry. Horses, cows and sheep will also eat it with relish."

The weed was sometimes called 'loveman', which might be a loose translation of the Greek *philanthropon* or 'loving humankind'. Swedish botanist Carl Linnaeus (1707–78) called the plant *'aparine'*, originating from the Greek *aparo*, 'to seize', likely referring to its clinging qualities. Its botanical title *Galium* is thought to derive from the Greek 'milk', referring to its ability to curdle milk.

FOOD

Cleavers traditionally, like many common weeds, was known to make an excellent potherb. It was a useful green in medieval kitchens because the hardy plant could sometimes be picked in frost or snow, despite its aforementioned seasonal nature. In today's herbal kitchen, young tender shoots can be boiled and buttered as a vegetable or left to cool and added to salad. The leaves and stems can be made into soups and stews. Foragers should take note, however, that the prickly hairs make the uncooked plant difficult to eat, so it's best eaten cooked. Richard Mabey (1978) encourages beginners not to be intimidated by Cleavers' hook-like bristles, which once boiled will melt away and lose their "forbidding sharpness".

As for its flavour, Grieve (1931) described it as bitter and astringent. Other texts hint at Cleavers' unpalatable taste: "In Munster it was said of a greedy person that: *d'iosfaidh se an gharbhach* – 'he would even eat Cleavers'" (Mac Coitir, 2015).

The whole plant is rich in vitamin C, so it brings added value to hearty meals like warmed vegetable salads. However, Henriette Kress's *Practical Herbs* (2011) suggests that a variant of Cleavers called Lady's Bedstraw (*Galium verum*) has a higher content of vitamin C than *G. aparine*.

Gabrielle Hatfield (2007) introduces Cleavers as Goosegrass – a wholly nutritious plant largely for culinary use, also "fed to poultry to fatten them". What made geese fat made humans lean it seems. Cleavers has long been recommended as a slimming aid. Gerard wrote in the sixteenth century: "Women do usually make pottage of Clevers with a little mutton and Otemeale, to cause lanknesse, and keep them from fatnesse." Hatfield speculates that its perceived slimming effects may be explained by its diuretic properties.

John Evelyn mentioned in his *Acetaria: A Discourse of Sallets* (1699) that the young shoots of Cleavers were mixed with nettle tops to make a healthful, and most likely cleansing, 'Lenten pottage'. In Ireland, eating the leaves of Cleavers was said to make fat people thin.

A thirteenth-century Cleavers beverage is described in the book Meddygon Myddfai (Pughe, 1861):

> "Take the whole herb, leaves, blossoms, and seed included, (as the season may be,) and pound them together well: then put in an unglazed earthenware vessel, and fill it up without pressing them; then pour thereon as much as it will admit of pure spring water, and let it stand a night. Some say that it is best that a quarter of it should be sea water, or water salted as much as sea water, for the first week of drinking; then ceasing from the salt water, it should be taken fresh as the only drink for nine weeks. It is wonderful how strong and healthy you will become in that time."

Cleavers coffee is a traditional countryside beverage and has been used, for example, in Britain, Ireland and Sweden. This is not surprising given that the plant belongs to the coffee family. Its ripe fruits are lightly toasted, then ground and brewed in a cafetiere. The taste is similar to the instant chicory drinks you can purchase in health shops. Tea lovers, however, "may delight in Cleavers", wrote Grieve (1931), for the whole plant "gives a decoction equal to tea". For iced drinks, Cleavers can be frozen for later use. Simply pick, juice and freeze into ice cube trays.

As a cosmetic herb, a decoction of the plant, or a tea (as is the custom in China) can be used under the arms as a deodorant. In addition, drinking a cup of Cleavers tea is said to clear up skin problems, thanks to its blood-purifying properties.

In the first century AD, the Greek physician Dioscorides mentioned its use by shepherds as a sieve to strain the (animal) hairs out of milk. The shoots, when bound together, may still be used as a sieve for kitchen use, wrote Hatfield. Grieve (1931) also tells us that: "Linnaeus reported the same use being made of it in Sweden, in country districts, as a filter to strain milk; the stalks are still used thus in Sweden".

The herb's milk-curdling properties have been used to make kosher cheese in some Jewish communities. Hatfield (2007) also tells us that: "Dairy farmers used the juice as a vegetable rennet for making cheese and junket."

RECIPES

Cleavers & Aubergine Bake

- 650g sliced (rounds) aubergine
- 150g cleavers tips
- 2 onions (sliced)
- 2 garlic cloves (chopped)
- 2 tbsp mixed herbs
- 1 tin of tomatoes
- 500ml cheese sauce
- 2 tsps tomato puree
- salt
- water

Slice aubergine, then lightly oil the slices, now grill them for 2 minutes on high until wilted, turning occasionally. Steam fry the cleavers straight from being washed, do not bother to shake dry, then set aside. Sauté the onions and garlic until translucent, then add the tin tomatoes, mixed herbs, a pinch of salt and the tomato puree. Stir and simmer for 15 minutes. In the meantime make up your cheese sauce. When both the sauces are ready, layer a dish with tomato sauce, aubergine, cleavers and cheese sauce, then repeat until all used up finishing with a layer of cheese sauce on top. Pop in the oven at 180 degrees and bake until piping hot and bubbling, about 30 minutes. Serves: 2

Cleavers Soup

- 300g of Cleavers tips
- 2 medium potatoes
- 2 large shallots
- 300ml soured cream
- 1 litre of vegetable stock

Dice the potatoes and chop the shallots and fry together until shallots are translucent. Add the stock and bring to a simmering boil, then finely chop the wild greens and add to the pan. Reduce the heat and simmer until the potato is cooked. Blend until smooth, then stir in the soured cream and serve.

Cleavers Kedgeree

1 cup very young Cleavers shoots (no more than 6 cms high)

- 1 small onion / shallot - chopped
- Butter or oil
- Ground turmeric - pinch
- 1 cup rice - cooked
- 1 hard-boiled egg - chopped
- Salt and pepper
- Cayenne or paprika [optional]

Roughly chop the Cleavers. Fry the onion until it softens. Then stir in a pinch of turmeric and continue cooking for another minute. Add the rice and chopped cleavers, some seasoning, and the optional sprinkle of cayenne or paprika. Continue cooking the mixture for a couple of minutes then add the egg and mix in. Keep on the heat for another minute or so to allow the egg to heat through, then serve.

MEDICINE

Cleavers is one of the humbler plants of folk medicine, being helpful for many conditions, but not excelling in any particular remedy. Grieve noted in 1931 that the herb was, as it still is, "extolled for its powers" as a purifier of the blood, although it does not appear to rival burdock in this area. Like many spring weeds, its greenness was valued as a spring tonic to strengthen and cleanse the body. Gabrielle Hatfield recalls a fizzy, beer-like drink made from nettles and Goosegrass (Cleavers) in East Anglia, England, which was drunk as a countryside tonic.

Dioscorides recommended Cleavers for fighting fatigue, which may in part be due to its soothing effect and application as an aid to restful sleep. In old English herbals, it was recommended as a remedy for snake and insect bites (Gerard) and for earache (Culpeper).

Records of its use in parts of Britain suggest it was widely employed for colds, cuts and wounds, and sometimes for snake bites. There are also records of its use for cancerous tumours, boils, warts and rheumatism. Grieve wrote that the plant was used for scalds and burns in the fourteenth century. It was an ancient gypsy remedy for cancer, and one of the plants used for abortion by gypsies in former Yugoslavia.

Peter Wyse Jackson (2014) noted Allen and Hatfield's observations of Cleavers' use in Irish folk medicine as a cure for tumours, burns, stomach ache, whooping cough and inflammatory bowel conditions in children. He also recorded its use for kidney problems, gonorrhoea, ulcers, cancerous growths, and skin complaints like impetigo.

Allen and Hatfield themselves (2004) acknowledged that despite Cleavers' wide-ranging application in folk medicine, its use was restricted to a few places around the British Isles. This might, in part, be due to its seasonal nature – unlike nettle, it wasn't widely available year-round – and in part due to substitution by similar herbs of greater effectiveness.

Hatfield (2007) said: "In official medicine it was used to treat a wide variety of illnesses, among them burns and bites, dropsy, gravel and stone (urinary stones) and scrofula (glandular tuberculosis)." However, she added:

> "In folk medicine the plant was associated with completely different ailments: it was a first-aid treatment for cuts and scratches and, in particular, leg ulcers. It was also widely used to treat coughs, colds, wounds and occasionally tumours."

Around the world, Cleavers has been widely regarded as a helpful, cleansing herb. In Native American herbalism, it was a cure for kidney ailments, urinary disorders, infections and itching. The Chippewa used Cleavers as a laxative and for dermatitis; Fox Indians used it as an emetic; the Ojibwa and Penobscot used it as a diuretic for kidney and urinary problems; the Iroquois used it for itch and poison ivy; and the Micmac used it for gonorrhea and kidney ailments. In the Mahabharata Range, also known as the Lesser Himalayas or Lower Himalayan Range, a paste is made from the fresh leaves and applied to wounds, and an extract of the leaves is used to treat jaundice. In the East Indies, juiced Cleavers is taken as a remedy for gonorrhea.

With a long history of general use in folk medicine, Cleavers is still widely used by modern herbalists. It's indicated for a number of conditions ranging from skin problems, such as eczema, psoriasis, ulcers and wounds, to serious diseases, such as cancer, tuberculosis and scarlet fever. A tea, in particular, is said to be effective for psoriasis. As Grieve said in 1931: "Modern herbalists and homeopaths still recognise the value of this herb". She gave some simple home uses: a soothing tea for insomnia, and a face wash for sunburn and freckles. She also referred to its use as an ointment to treat cancerous growths and ulcers.

Cleavers has also been recommended for 'hysteria', perhaps meaning anxiety, and epilepsy.

Some present-day herbals list its use for regulating menstruation in such cases as amenorrhoea, or infrequent periods, and for conditions such as obesity and water retention. The plant retains its former use as a treatment for kidney stones and for itching, such as that caused by poison ivy. The leaves and flowers can be taken for headaches, migraine and sinusitis.

What qualifies Cleavers as such a versatile healer, you might ask? It is thought to be antibacterial, astringent and anti-inflammatory; to act as a diuretic and laxative; and to be able to stimulate the immune system.

Herbalpedia (2014) mentions its value as a tonic for swollen glands, perhaps relating to its anti-inflammatory properties.

> "It would be used in swollen glands anywhere in the body and especially in tonsillitis and in adenoid trouble. It eliminates excess

fluid, counteracts inflammations, and urinary infections, hepatitis and venereal disease."

Kress (2011) and others have recorded the plant as a lymphatic remedy that is useful for inflamed lymph nodes and cysts, as well as sores, blisters, slow-healing wounds, scar tissue and eczema; although these references largely refer to 'bedstraws', perhaps indicating *G. verum* rather than *G. aparine*.

Angela Paine (2006) explained that a sluggish lymphatic system, which can result in poor skin and joint problems, can be treated with Cleavers. Once normal lymphatic function has been restored, so is a feeling of general energy and wellness. She noted: "Sometimes when we are particularly low and depleted of energy our lymph nodes become swollen and inflamed. This is called lymphadenitis. Clivers is the best remedy for lymphadenitis."

Methods of use are varied, as is expected of a wild herb but usually include infusions, juices, tinctures, teas and compresses. Kress has added to this list a maceration of the herb in water.

In modern medicine the plant, like most weeds, is neglected, though a note in the *British Medical Journal* by a Dublin physician (1883) reports how surprised he was to the efficacy of Goosegrass (Cleavers) pulp when applied to a large leg ulcer that other doctors had been unable to cure.

> "This paste, which has an acrid taste and slightly acrid smell, is made up into a large poultice, applied to the ulcer, and secured with a bandage. It is renewed three times a day. Its action appears to be a slight steady stimulant, and powerful promoter of healthy granulation. Its effect in this most unhopeful case was decisive and plain to all. Healthy action ensued, and has since steadily contin-

ued; and, after a month of treatment, both ulcers have been reduced to considerably less than half their original size. If this action continue, which I have no reason to doubt, the cure will be accomplished within a measurable and short period."

In veterinary medicine, the plant is considered generally useful for horses. Research into its chemistry has found a mild laxative effect in mice. Its plant tannins, as in all plants, are known to be astringent.

SAFETY NOTE

Some herbals suggest that the juice of the plant should be avoided by diabetics, although Barnes, Phillipson and Anderson (2013) stated there's no evidence to support this. Indeed, there is little scientific information to support Cleavers use in herbal medicine altogether, and not much data about its safety profile; therefore it has been suggested that excessive use is best avoided. In addition, it may cause severe skin irritation, according to Karalliedde and Gawarammana (2007).

BOTANICAL PROFILE

Scientific Name: *Galium aparine.*

Family: Rubiaceae.

Botanical Description

Height: up to 0.9–1m. Stems: long with tiny hooks that stick to clothing and fur. Flowers: clusters of small white flowers. Leaves: whorled, willow-shaped leaves around 2–7cm long and 0.5–1cm wide, with tiny hooks and sometimes with hairy margins. Fruit:

globe-shaped, greenish brown to black nutlike fruits. Foliage: vine-like growth.

Flowers: April to September.

Status: Annual. Native.

Habitat: Cultivated land, hedgerows, scrub.

Cleavers (*Galium aparine*)

4

DANDELION

The Dandelion is a very common garden weed, scattering lawns everywhere with bright yellow flowers in spring. Once a cure-all of herbal medicine, it more recently became regarded as a nuisance to be vigorously dug up by gardeners. Today the Dandelion is enjoying a comeback as a cosmopolitan weed used in various herbal remedies and culinary dishes worldwide.

Throughout literature, the Dandelion's bold beauty has drawn comparisons with the sun and the lion. Its common name may derive from the French *'dent de lion'* ('lion's tooth'), or from the earlier Latin *'dens leonis'*, which may be due to its long white tap root, the sunny hue of its flower, or its jagged, teeth-like leaves. Mrs Grieve, in *A Modern Herbal* (1931), suggested that the leaves resemble a lion's open jaw more than a single tooth, that its long white root is suggestive of a fang, and its yellow flowers could be likened to the golden teeth of the heraldic lion.

It's not hard to imagine the Dandelion as an emblem of the sun, with its bright flower head like a miniature star, or the shaggy yellow petals as a lion's mane. Richard Folkard (1892) stated: "Certainly the appearance of the Dandelion-flower is very suggestive of the ancient representations of the Sun." But not everyone is convinced that this is how it got its name.

Grieve suggested the name *Taraxacum* comes from the Greek *taraxos*, meaning disorder, and *akos*, meaning remedy, due to the plant's usefulness in folk medicine. Other sources suggest the Latin name has its origins in the Arabic word *tharakhchakon*, used to describe a similar plant and dating from the end of the Middle Ages. Indeed, according to Grieve, the first mention of Dandelion in medicine is in the texts of tenth- and eleventh-century Arabian physicians, where it is referred to as *Taraxacon* and described as a wild endive.

FOOD

Dandelion has been included in cookbooks on wild foods since ancient times, and it could become popular again thanks to its availability as a cheap, plentiful and nutritious ingredient. It's still consumed widely in the commercially-produced fizzy drink 'Dandelion and burdock', made in the north of England.

In Flanders and south Holland it was once said that Shrove Tuesday, or Pancake Day, was the best evening on which to bake. "'*Zy heeft het zoo druk, als de pan te vastelavond*' ('She's as busy as the pan on Shrove Tuesday'), were used to describe someone who was extremely busy, especially in the kitchen." (Cleene and Lejeune, 2002). The humble Dandelion had a place at the baker's table on this night, being bleached along with tansy and used in gingerbread.

From root to tip, Dandelion has played a part in culinary delights around the world. The American Indians, for example, made good use of the versatile plant in many dishes. The Meskwaki cooked it with pork, and the Menomini cooked it with vinegar and maple sap. In parts of India today, the roots and rhizomes are incorporated in raw salads, cooked as a vegetable side dish, or made into soups. In Lebanon Dandelion leaves are gathered as part of a spring festivity, to be used in little pasties and salads.

Samuel Thayer (2006) described the benefits of Dandelion coffee, which has been drunk across Europe since ancient times. This healthy drink lacks only one component. "I suspect that if Dandelion were endowed with caffeine and coffee was deprived of this stimulant, the world would drink billions of dollars' worth of Dandelion and the coffee tree would be an unknown component of African highland flora." In World War II, Dandelion roots were used as an 'emergency coffee' made in Co. Cork, in Ireland, although the drink may actually have a sedative effect which can aid a good night's sleep.

Alongside its popular use as a coffee substitute, Dandelion leaves and roots were dried and smoked as a substitute for tobacco.

Dandelion leaves are considered to be highly nutritious. In past times, before commercially produced groceries were available year-round, Dandelions provided a local source of fresh greens. Thayer (2006) said:

> "These nutrient-packed greens were strongly craved – and with good reason. Dandelion greens are extremely high in vitamins A, K, and beta carotene. They are also high in vitamins E, C, thiamine, riboflavin, B6, folate, and the minerals calcium, iron, potassium, and manganese."

In his wartime *Kitchen Front* broadcasts, BBC Radio's Dr Charles Hill advised people to supplement their rations with Dandelions, although he apparently failed to increase the number of 'Dandelion-eaters' around the country.

The Dandelion is considered among the most useful nutritional plants of India, where it's known variously as *dulal* (Hindi), *pathardi* (Gujarati), *dudli, baran, radam, dudh-batthal, kanphul, shamukei* (in Punjab), and *hand* (in Kashmir). All parts of the plants are used. The leaves are valued as an antiscorbutic vegetable (rich in vitamin C) and the flowers are pickled for various uses. Both leaves and flowers can be harvested for incorporation in beer, wines and stouts.

In the temperate parts of the Himalayas, and in Khasi, Mishmi, the South Indian hills and Gujarat, Dandelion leaves are foraged before the plant flowers and boiled as nutritious greens – they contain phosphorus, calcium, iron and vitamin C.

In Asian cooking, the leaves are used like lettuce, boiled, made into soup or fried as in Vietnam. In Japan they are cooked 'nituke' style, similar to steaming, in soy sauce. In China the Dandelion grows so prolifically from lawns to waysides that it is commonly included in lists of edible plants.

Though the virtues of Dandelion in cooking are expounded in many texts, its bitter taste is also cautioned against. John Kallas (2010) said: "Many people today want to eat fresh raw foods. In order for that to work with Dandelion, you either have to love their bitterness, or you must work it into other foods that can dilute the bitterness." It's thought best to collect the young leaves in early spring when the bitterness is milder.

Dandelion flowers are traditional fare in country cookbooks for desserts, teas and wines. The flower buds can be stirred into pancake batter, omelette mixtures and fritters. The open flowers can be baked in cakes, such as the Arabic *yublo*, or made into jelly known as 'Dandelion honey'. The pollen can be sprinkled on food for decoration and colouring. From the sweet to the sour, there is still a strong custom of pickling the flower buds in the Czech Republic and Slovakia.

Dandelion blossoms make a delicious country wine, and a beer can be made from the whole plant before it flowers. The plant is also one of over thirty herbs and spices used to make the non-alcoholic beverage Norfolk Punch, originally formulated by the monks of Norfolk in England.

There is an indirect, but valuable, use for the plant in food production, of interest to fruit farmers. Dandelions give off ethylene gas, which is beneficial in ripening fruit, and fruit farmers may allow Dandelions to grow in their orchards for this reason. This has an additional benefit in that Dandelions are a year-round source of nectar and pollen for bees; thus they assist both pollinator and fruit farmer, and contribute to the beekeeper's honey crop.

RECIPES

Dandelion Root Coffee

Dig up a 2 kg of dandelion roots and wash. Slice the dandelion roots into small pieces (0.5cm to 1cm), and then arrange on a baking tray. Allow to air dry for 60 minutes. Roast the dandelion root for 60 minutes on 325°F/170°C/150 Fan. The roots need to be brown and dried right through. Cool then store in an airtight container.

Put 30g of dandelion coffee grinds into 600ml of boiling water and simmer on low for 30 minutes. Serve black or with milk and honey.

A Simple Dandelion Salad

- 250g baby beetroots in mild malt vinegar
- 130g goat's cheese
- 2 small cox apples
- 1 handful of washed small Dandelion leaves
- 3cm piece of ginger
- olive oil
- cracked black pepper

Grate the apple along with the peeled ginger and mix together. Next dice the beetroots and goat's cheese and mix with the apple and ginger. Finely slice the dandelion leaves lengthways and fold into the salad mixture along with a few glugs of olive oil. Season with cracked black pepper.

Dandelion Dressing

- 10 cherry tomatoes
- 30 young dandelion leaves (roughly chopped)
- 3tbs Greek yoghurt
- 3tbs lemon juice
- 3 garlic cloves (crushed)
- 1tbs date syrup or maple syrup
- salt & black pepper

Rub oil over the tomatoes, place whole on a baking tray and sprinkle with a little salt. Roast the cherry tomatoes at 180 degrees until the skins are just splitting. Allow to cool, then arrange them on a plate. Wash and roughly chop the dandelion greens, and put in a bowl, then add the garlic. Next add the yoghurt, lemon juice and date syrup, then mix all together with a fork, then spoon over roasted tomatoes.

MEDICINE

Until as recently as the 1930s, root diggers in East Anglia, England made a living from selling Dandelion roots. Gabrielle Hatfield (2007) wrote: "So common was this practice that a special 'green-herb' rate was charged for transporting them by train to London. Nowadays, the Dandelion root used by herbalists is mostly imported."

In folk medicine, Dandelion was renowned for its diuretic effects, and drinking a decoction was thought to treat gall stones, kidney stones, obesity, cellulite and water retention. However, it was also thought to have the less desirable effect of causing some to wet their beds. For this reason, in France it was called *'pissenlit'* or *'pisse au lit'*, meaning 'bed wetter'. Other nicknames in the UK were 'pee-in-bed' and 'wet-the-bed'. Children were told not to pick Dandelions because it could make them wet the bed, although Hatfield suggested this may have been to prevent the plant staining their hands and clothes brown.

Several records around the world suggest the Dandelion may be used as a tonic for the stomach and liver. Among the edible wild plants of Vietnam, it's valued for its diuretic and detoxifying properties. It's used as a liver tonic, appetite stimulant and blood regulator, to treat boils and lesions, and to treat insect and snake bites. In Indian herbal medicine, the roots and rhizomes are prepared as a mild laxative and can be used as both a stomach tonic and liver stimulant. In Wales, the Physicians of Myddfai used Dandelion to treat fever, for instance in malaria patients, because, they reasoned, the root of the plant stimulated the liver infected by the disease. It's unknown whether the remedy was effective.

The list of ailments that Dandelion has been used to treat in Ireland is probably the most exhaustive. The plant's abundant growth is matched only by its reputation as a cure-all of herbal medicine, used to treat stomach and liver complaints, diabetes, external cancers, heart problems, anaemia, respiratory ailments, consumption (tuberculosis), toothache, broken bones and sprains, sore eyes, cuts and nervousness. It was even used in folk medicine to treat animals, from calves suffering from liver complaints or diarrhoea to horses with various diseases and pains.

Culpeper (1653) added to the list of complaints treated by Dandelion: "It helps to procure rest and sleep to bodies distempered by the heat of ague fits." As late as the nineteenth century, the *British Pharmaceutical Codex of 1914* recommended Dandelion for jaundice, dropsy, liver or lung disease, and as a digestive, while modern herbalists still recommend it as a tonic for arthritis, constipation, gall bladder problems and skin conditions.

Another principal use for Dandelion was treating warts with the juice from any part of the plant. The juice was rubbed on the wart and left to dry until the wart apparently shrunk and disappeared.

Food was often prescribed as medicine in herbal traditions. Dandelion sandwiches were considered beneficial because of the action of chewing and sucking on the leaves to treat tuberculosis, bronchitis and indigestion. The young leaves in sandwiches of bread and butter sprinkled with salt were also reportedly delicious.

The fortifying powers of Dandelion wine led to extraordinary claims. "This extract from *The Times*, 23 January 1951: 'Mr William Weeds, of Caunsall, near Kidderminster, who was 100 last November, died yesterday. For 75 years he has taken a daily glass of Dandelion wine, and contended that this beverage enabled his grandmother to live to be 103" (quoted in Watts, 2007).

In modern medicine, there is little research into Dandelion's clinical properties, despite its valuable reputation in herbal medicine.

Angela Paine (2006), however, described a few tests that have been carried out using Dandelion-derived drugs on small animals, summarised below.

In 1974, Racz-Kotilla and his research group investigated the diuretic effect of Dandelion leaves and roots on rats and mice. They discovered that the leaves were more powerful than the roots and that an extract of the leaf had the same diuretic effect as the pharmaceutical drug frusemide. The leaf extract had the additional benefit of not depleting the body of potassium, unlike the drug, which can cause side effects such as muscle spasms. Frusemide may be prescribed by doctors for high blood pressure, whereas herbalists may suggest Dandelion juice or tincture to lower blood pressure. As ever, it is advised to first seek a diagnosis and prescription for any condition from a health professional before self-medicating with herbal remedies.

In 1977, Vogel in Germany showed that Dandelion root can stimulate the flow of bile in the body, which stimulates the digestive system and liver. This supports the plant's traditional use as a tonic for these body systems. Paine listed several scientific studies researching Dandelion between 1985 and 1998 that demonstrated its medical properties. The roots were shown to lower blood sugar in rabbits (Akhtar, 1985), to reduce inflammation in rats (Mascolo, 1987), and to enhance immunity in animals (Luo, 1993). A research group in Korea tested Dandelion in vitro and also found it had a stimulating effect on immune cells (Kim, 1998).

Thus, concludes Paine, science may have shown how Dandelion actually works, but the effects they found are what herbalists have always observed.

SAFETY NOTE

Traditional usage of Dandelion in herbal medicine is wide-ranging; however, it may cause allergic reactions in people who are sensitive to plants of the same family (Asteraceae) such as ragweed and daisies.

BOTANICAL PROFILE

Scientific Name: *Taraxacum officinale.*

Family: Compositae.

Botanical Description

Height: various from 1–30 cm depending on the maturity of the plant and environmental conditions. Flowers: composite bright yellow flowers. Leaves: a rosette of large tapering jagged green leaves; the leaves are sometimes compared to a lion's tooth or jaw. Root: long tapering white root in older established plants, thinner roots and rhizomes in younger plants.

Flowers: March to October.

Status: Perennial. Native.

Habitat: Cultivated land, grassland, hedgerows, meadow, river banks, roadsides, short turf, wasteland, dunes & dune slacks.

Dandelion (*Taraxacum officinale*)

5
GARLIC MUSTARD

Learning the history of a plant somehow makes it more attractive in culinary use, but Garlic Mustard has attracted few stories. Though unrelated to garlic, *Alliaria petiolata* gives off a garlic-like smell when its leaves are bruised or chopped.

A common wild herb in Britain and Ireland, Garlic Mustard is found across Europe, where it appears largely forgotten, and it was introduced to North America, where it's largely seen as an invasive weed.

With its rosette of heart-shaped leaves crowned by bright-white, cross-shaped flowers, one would imagine it to be a plant steeped in fairy romance and early Christian legend. Instead, this wild herb is missing its place in folklore.

FOOD

The release of a garlic smell and taste when the leaves are crushed led to the use of Garlic Mustard as an alternative to true garlic. It also made an excellent savoury salad green and potherb. However, it might well have been an acquired taste. Joseph Tom Burgess wrote in 1868: "It has been used as a salad herb, boiled as a table vegetable, and made into sauce in the same manner as mint; but it is only tolerable in the absence of all other vegetables." One of its common names was 'sauce-alone'; 'alone' derived from 'ail', meaning 'garlic'.

On the other hand, Gerard (1597) wrote that it was good with salt fish, and Scottish botanist John Loudon in 1824 in An Encyclopedia of Gardening says: "It is occasionally used as a salad; boiled as a pot-herb, or introduced in sauces. Neill observes, that, 'when gathered as it approaches the flowering state, boiled separately, and then eaten with boiled mutton, it certainly forms a most desirable pot-herb; and to any kind of salted meat, an excellent green'."

For those whose taste leans more towards the plant's bitter-sweet aromatic flavour, Garlic Mustard adds an interesting twist to mint sauce, pesto or mustard. It is a good addition to stews and casseroles. Richard Mabey (1978) suggested it as a garlic flavouring for those who like garlic, "but only in moderation". He particularly recommended it as a 'mint' sauce for lamb, with hawthorn buds, vinegar and sugar.

François Couplan (1998) prefers to eat the wild herb raw, feeling that the leaves lose their garlic aroma after cooking, whereas they retain a bitter-sweet aftertaste in salad. The leaves can be eaten without fuss in bread and butter, according to Stephen Facciola in *Cornucopia II* (also 1998). Indeed, it has been said that the countryside habit of using Garlic Mustard leaves in sandwiches with salted meat and lettuce led to its name 'sauce alone'.

As a sauce or condiment, Garlic Mustard complements bland egg dishes, makes an interesting side vegetable for salty meat such as pork chops, and perhaps makes a tasty stuffing for mushrooms. The seeds can be used to spice dishes or the seed pods eaten raw.

In North America, Garlic Mustard is often labelled an invasive weed. Samuel Thayer (2006) wrote:

> "It was the rogue vegetable, the evil plant, the wildflower to end all wildflowers. First posses were formed to fight it, then armies were raised. Propaganda was written and distributed to stir up the public against this evil foreign invader. Yes –Garlic Mustard– that despicable displacer of our beloved woodland flora. You cannot utter the very name among wildflower watchers without hearing the murmurs and echoes of contempt."

According to Thayer, Garlic Mustard thrives on forest floors and rapidly crowds out native flora. He noted: "It is also *allelopathic*– chemically inhibiting the growth of competing plants." To do his part to eradicate the wild vegetable, he picks the young succulent shoots before they flower and largely discards the leaves, while chopping the sweet, juicy stalks to eat raw as snacks, in salads, boiled or steamed like asparagus, or made into soup. While Thayer prefers the milder flavour of the stems, he accedes the flower buds and leafy tops may be used in roast beef sandwiches. He once tried making mustard from the seeds, which tasted "really nasty" – but noted that on the bright side "I destroyed all those seeds".

James Duke (2002) is more generous in his view of Garlic Mustard, even giving it a place among his "Christmas greens".

RECIPES

Garlic Mustard and Blue Cheese Pasta

- 200g garlic mustard stems
- 30g butter
- 25g plain flour

- 400ml milk
- 100g Saint Agur blue cheese (or equivalent)
- pasta
- cracked black pepper

Chop the garlic mustard stems then bring a pan of water to the boil, place the stems into it and bring back to the boil, then drain and set aside. Now bring a pan of water to the boil and cook enough pasta for two people. While it is cooking put the butter into a small saucepan, and on low heat wait until it has melted, then add the flour and cook stirring all the time for about a minute. Make sure the flour does not burn. Then remove from the heat and slowly add the milk a little at a time making sure to stir continuously. Return to the heat and keep adding splashes of milk until it has all been added and is going thick. Then simmer the sauce for a further minute, and when done add the crumbled/chopped blue cheese, and stir until melted into the sauce. Mix together the garlic mustard stems, pasta and sauce and serve.

Garlic Mustard and Cauliflower Cakes

- 250g cauliflower
- 250g potatoes
- 75g young garlic mustard leaf
- 10g fresh tarragon
- 10g dried, powdered seaweed greens
- 2tbsp olive oil
- 1tbsp ground toasted glutinous rice powder

Toast the glutinous rice and the grind it in an electric spice/nut grinder or use a mortar and pestle. In a food processor blitz the raw cauliflower until the consistency of rice and transfer to a bowl.

Halve the potatoes and boil until cooked (about 15 minutes). Mash, then and add to the cauliflower.

Next, finely slice and chop the wild garlic and put in the bowl with the cauliflower along with chopped tarragon, seaweed greens, olive oil and toasted rice. Mix thoroughly together. I use my hands. Form into cakes, and place on an oiled baking tray or parchment paper. Cook at 170°C (fan-assisted), 190°C (regular), 325°F, gas mark 3 for 20-30 minutes depending on how thick your cakes are.

Smoked Tofu and Garlic Mustard

- 250 g smoked tofu (cubed)
- 2 handfuls of finely sliced young garlic mustard leaves
- 1 handful of finely sliced stinging nettle leaves
- 3tbsp coriander seeds
- 1/4tsp umami powder
- 1/2tsp ground ginger/fresh grated ginger
- 3tbsp sesame oil
- 1 handful of cashew nuts
- rice vinegar (to taste)
- Tamari/soy sauce (to taste)
- 1tbsp honey
- 1 lemon (juiced + lemon zest to taste)

Heat sesame oil until very hot, then add the coriander seeds and cashew nuts, fry for 30 seconds, then remove from oil and put aside.

Mix together the sea salt, cracked black pepper, umami & ginger. Coat the smoked tofu, then cook for 3 minutes.

Just before the end of cooking the tofu add the sliced wild greens, rice vinegar, tamari/soya sauce, honey & finally the lemon juice.

MEDICINE

Garlic Mustard is absent from British pharmacopeia, according to herbalist Gabrielle Hatfield (2007). Its last mention was in 1838 as a treatment for leg ulcers. A couple of centuries earlier, Culpeper (1653) recommended its use for leg ulcers, (Pechey, 1694) wrote: "The seeds rubbed and put into the nose, provokes sneezing and purges the head." The English empiric doctor William Salmon (1710) recommended it for coughs and colds. John Gerard (1597), a century earlier still, said Garlic Mustard was a good cure for colic and kidney stones. In the Middle Ages, the herb was used as an antiseptic and to encourage sweating.

More broadly in folk medicine, the leaves were chewed to alleviate mouth ulcers, perhaps because of the plant's antiseptic qualities. This was also a remedy for sore throats and gums.

The large, fresh, green leaves of Garlic Mustard were applied to wounds, or, in a cure recorded in Somerset, England, rubbed on feet to relieve cramp. Hatfield (2007) wrote: "Within living memory, the plant was boiled and made into an ointment for treating bruises and sores." However, Allen and Hatfield (2004) suggested in *Medicinal Plants in Folk Tradition* that its medicinal use was restricted to the south-eastern quarter of England, where Garlic Mustard itself was once confined.

Herbalpedia described Garlic Mustard as a "pungent, stimulating herb that clears infection, encourages healing, and is expectorant and anti-inflammatory, diuretic, vulnerary, antiputrefactive…", suggesting a wide range of uses, from treating coughs and colds to healing and cleansing the body.

In modern herbal medicine, its stems and leaves are considered antiasthmatic and antiseptic, which indicates its use for conditions such as bronchitis and asthma, or for bites and stings. The plant's other medical properties suggest it's useful for expelling worms (a vermifuge), remedying scurvy (antiscorbutic), encouraging sweating (diaphoretic), and healing wounds such as ulcers (vulnerary). It might also be recommended for eczema, neuralgia, rheumatism and gout.

A medicinal preparation of the leaves can be used to warm the stomach and aid digestion, while the juice is said to be antibacterial and can be boiled with honey to treat coughs and phlegm.

Its most mentioned active constituent in herbals is glucoside (sinigrin) essential oil.

As a member of the mustard family, which includes cabbage, cauliflower, broccoli, brussels sprouts, mustard and watercress, Garlic Mustard could be among those vegetables whose consumption might help to prevent cancer. Duke (2002) wrote: "In its new Designer Food Program, the NCI is including this weed for study because it embraces the chemistry of both the mustard and garlic, both with well-deserved chemopreventive reputations." It shares cancer-preventing chemicals isothiocyanates, from the mustard family, and allyl sulfides, from the garlic family. A 1977 study by Zennie and Ogzewalla, found Garlic Mustard leaves have twice the amount of cancer-preventing beta-carotene as spinach.

SAFETY NOTE

Garlic Mustard is apparently "palatable to livestock", which suggests another means to manage its spread on the borders of fields and woodlands. An unfortunate side effect of this, however, is that it might lend a disagreeable flavour to cow's milk and an unpleasant taste to poultry meat.

BOTANICAL PROFILE

Scientific Name: *Alliaria petiolata.*

Family: Brassicaceae.

Botanical Description

Height: up to 120cm. Flowers: small, bright-white flowers with cross-shaped petals. Leaves: large green and slightly toothed leaves, sometimes described as heart-shaped. Stalk: grows straight and is smoothed, rounded with scattered hairs.

Flowers: April to June.

Status: Biennial. Native.

Habitat: Hedgerows, woodland, waste places.

Garlic Mustard (*Alliaria petiolata*)

6
GROUND ELDER

It is unlikely that Ground Elder is native to Britain. Several authorities suggest it was introduced to this country by medieval monks who cultivated it as a medicinal plant. Other sources say that it arrived with the Romans and made itself useful as a potherb and as a treatment for gout. Whatever its origins, Ground Elder outstayed its welcome and became a nuisance weed reluctant to give up its place in the herb garden. Its creeping, stubborn root system earned the name 'jump about' and 'farmer's plague' in some parts of Britain because it spread vigorously and rapidly. Herbalist and botanist John Gerard (1597) observed:

> "Herbe Gerard growth of itself in gardens without setting or sowing and is so fruitful in its increase that when it hath once taken roote, it will hardly be gotten out againe, spoiling and getting every yeare more ground, to the annoying of better herbe".

Richard le Strange tells us the Latin name *'Aegopodium'* is derived from the Greek *'aigos'* or *'aix'* for 'goat' and *'pous'* or *'podium'* for 'foot', because of the shape of the leaves and from which it gets the common names of 'goat's foot' or 'goat's herb'. The species' name *'podagraria'* means 'good for gout' and is derived from *'podagra'*, meaning 'gout in the feet', referring to its treatment for gouty conditions.

Never was there so much folk history in the naming of a plant. Ground Elder's tendency to take hold of neglected habitats around buildings such as ecclesiastical ruins may have led to the names 'bishop's weed' and 'bishop's wort'. Its occurrence in these places was not entirely blown in by an opportunistic wind. The plant was cultivated by monks in the Middle Ages and given the name 'herb Gerard' as a dedication to St Gerard, a patron of gout sufferers (no relation to the famous sixteenth- to seventeenth-century botanist).

The saint was invoked in prayer when the herb was used to cure gout. The names 'bishop's weed' and 'bishop's wort' may equally refer to its specific use as a treatment for gouty conditions in the religious or wealthier classes with whom the disease was most often associated, though Donald Watts (2007) asked: "Were bishops particularly prone to gout? Probably so…" Richard Mabey (1978) suggested it was a practical name referring to the plant as a quick remedy for travellers' gout, because it grew outside monasteries and inns. Another plant growing in the medicinal garden called bullwort (*Ammi majus*) or bishop's weed may have lent its name to Ground Elder which it resembles in appearance.

A long list of names was associated with Ground Elder because of its resemblance to other plants. Its leaves looked like those of an elder tree, which earned it dog elder, dwarf elder and Dutch elder. Its foliage appeared like an ash tree growing across the ground, which earned it the name 'ashtree'.

FOOD

Ground Elder has a long tradition of being eaten as a potherb in Europe in the Middle Ages. That legacy survived in Sweden and Switzerland where it was collected for spring salads or cooked as a wild leafy vegetable. Linnaeus in the eighteenth century particularly recommended its young, tender leaves. In Anglo-Saxon Britain, the plant was used to clarify beers and may have been called 'gill' from the French *'guiller'*, meaning 'to ferment beer'.

In the markets of medieval Cracow, Poland, Ground Elder was once sold as a wild vegetable, but it is no longer eaten in the country despite being widespread. In some parts of the Ukraine, Ground Elder is still used as an ingredient of green *borscht*, a soup made of green vegetables. In north-west Germany, too, it may be collected in spring to make a green soup, or *grüne suppe*.

Today, the wild edible is detested by many gardeners as a persistent weed that stops other plants from growing near it. But one way to defeat the 'invader', suggested wild food forager Richard Mabey (1978), is to eat it. He recommended cooking like spinach for a tangy addition to the vegetable platter, but suggested serving in small quantities as it's "not to everyone's taste".

The strong flavour of Ground Elder, mentioned in many herbal texts, is a challenge for the cook. Some have said it is "quite tasty", others that it is "spicy and tolerable" and similar to spinach, and then there are those who find it simply "disagreeable". It is a plant that divides opinion. Grieve described the root as "pungent and aromatic" but disliked the distinct taste of the leaves, while Richard le Strange wrote that it can be disagreeable even when boiled. François Couplan, on the other hand, favours both the tender young leaves for making aromatic salads and the older leaves for their incense-like flavour when cooked, which he has recommended adding to gratin.

Nutritionally, the young leaves contain high amounts of vitamin C and are best picked in spring for use in salads and soups. And with a little imagination, Ground Elder can be added to a variety of dishes. Try adding the herb to soup, rice cakes, meat loaf and vegetarian meatballs. The secret to managing the plant's distinctive flavour, it suggests, is in the cooking: pick young leaves in spring, boil briefly in a small amount of salted water, and serve with a knob of butter.

Despite its strong flavour, Ground Elder has potential as a world economic plant and is listed in several texts as a nutritious wild edible. Its lack of use today is like many wild, leafy vegetables that are no longer eaten despite their historic importance in our diet and their value as a rich source of vitamins, folic acid and antioxidants.

Łukasz Łuczaj (2010) investigated the disappearance of wild greens from Polish diets since the nineteenth century. His study was in part based on an assumption that modern agriculture has sidelined local knowledge of wild plants and their former usefulness. In a survey that asked: "Do local people gather herbs in spring to be used in soups, particularly in famine years, and these herbs are?", Ground Elder (local names *'gier'* and *'barszcnica'*) was identified.

Civelek and Balkaya (2013) looked at the nutritional value of wild plants used as vegetables in the Black Sea Region of Turkey. Among nineteen plants studied, Ground Elder was again listed as a leafy vegetable that was boiled or roasted. Nutritionally, Ground Elder was found to contain nutrients such as ash, protein, phosphorus, potassium, magnesium and calcium; it scored highly in iron, manganese and zinc content. In fact, the study showed that many wild, leafy vegetables are higher in almost all nutrients than cultivated vegetables. More recent research has shown that Ground Elder leaves are an "excellent source of vitamins C, E, provitamin A, and xantophylls, which are important for human vision". Lack of data concerning the plant's toxicity means it's unlikely to be seen on supermarket shelves just yet, though it may have interesting potential as a future vegetable.

Research into the free-radical activity of *A. podagraria* and *Orlaya grandiflora* by Valyova and team (2016) found that extracts of both plants are natural sources of antioxidants. Given time, perhaps Ground Elder could be used as an antioxidant supplement to help fight oxidative damage to cells and reduce the incidence of diseases aggravated by free radicals.

While little use is made of Ground Elder as a food plant today, it is sometimes used as a fodder for pigs, and this use has given rise to another of its common names – 'pigweed'.

RECIPES

Ground Elder and Tempeh

- 2 good handfuls of ground elder leaves (stalks removed)
- 1 block of tempeh
- 3 good glugs of olive oil
- 1/4 cup of brown rice vinegar
- 2 tablespoons of tamari
- 2 crushed garlic cloves
- 1 red pepper
- a handful of chopped black olives

Cube the tempeh into small pieces. Combine the tempeh with the olive oil, brown rice vinegar, tamari and garlic and let sit for 3-10 hours (preferably stirring every hour). If you work away from home, cover the marinade and let it sit all day in the fridge. Turn the oven hob to high, and using a frying pan, quickly fry the tempeh and marinade mix until browned. Turn the heat down to mid-low, and add the red pepper and chopped black olives. Fry until the red pepper is cooked. About 5 minutes before serving, add the chopped Ground Elder and stir continuously until it looks like wilted spinach. Serve with vegetables of your choice.

Ground Elder Gazpacho Soup

- 1 handful of Ground Elder leaves
- 10 Nettle tops
- 4 medium sized tomatoes
- 1 glug of olive oil
- salt and pepper

Wash the Ground Elder leaves and Stinging Nettles. Chop the tomatoes. Put the Ground Elder leaves, Nettles and chopped tomatoes into a blender. Add a glug of olive oil. Now blend for about 3 minutes until smooth. If the mixture is too thick, add a little water until you have desired consistency. Add salt and pepper if you like. I prefer to not season this soup that much in order for the plant flavours to come out on their own.

Ground Elder Quiche

- 100g shallots (finely sliced)
- 100g blanched ground elder
- 3 eggs
- 150ml plain yoghurt
- 150ml whipping cream
- 50g grated cheese (your choice)
- nutmeg
- salt and pepper

Fry the onion until just translucent, then add in the ground elder leaves, stir and fry for a further minute. Whisk together the eggs, cheese, yoghurt, cream, nutmeg, salt & pepper. Heat oven to 200C/400F/Gas 6. Line a buttered 26cm quiche tin with pastry and pour in the filling. Bake for 30-35 minutes or until it has risen and golden brown.

MEDICINE

A conversation recorded about Ground Elder in Essex, England in the early twentieth century shows the plant's chequered past:

> "'That's a terrible useless plant, Fred! Serves no useful purpose I know of!' Fred then told me 'I only know one thing it is good for and that is to boil some of it up, and then when cold, use the solution on piles – it will cure them.'" (Essex Age Concern essay, 1991.)

Historically, Ground Elder wasn't widely used as a healing herb, but its uses were varied. The English herbalist John Parkinson said the herb reduced redness when drunk or topically applied and it was used as a remedy for people who "like to look pale."

Ground Elder tea was once drunk to treat eczema, and in East Anglia, the plant sap was rubbed on warts.

In Irish folk medicine, Ground Elder treated gout and the pain of sciatica. In the Orkney Islands, a decoction of the plant was taken for arthritis, and in the Scottish Highlands, an infusion was drunk to relieve aching joints and sciatica. In Britain, it was sometimes mixed with comfrey to make a first-aid ointment called 'greenstuff' which is mentioned in *Hatfield's Herbal* (2007): "The inventor of this ointment uses it on her family to this day".

Its primary use as a medicinal plant was to cure gout and to relieve pain and swelling. A German abbess and influential church mystic of the twelfth century, Hildegard of Bingen (1098–1179), knew Ground Elder as 'goutweed', or *'herba gicht'*, and, within the old doctrine of medicine, she valued its 'warm' and 'green' qualities. As a treatment for gout, Hildegard instructed that the plant should be mixed with its own seed, along with bear fat, oil and water to make an ointment that "immediately penetrates the skin, and the person's stormy period of gout will end". She also prescribed goutweed as a preventative treatment for digestive ills when taken with a potion of wine and honey:

> "Let whoever wishes to take a precaution so that the stomach does not become sick drink this same potion often and while it is cold; the stomach will remain healthy".

Gerard recommended Ground Elder's roots as a treatment for gout, swelling and inflammation, as did Culpeper(1653), who wrote:

> "It is not to be supposed Goutwort hath its name for nothing, but upon experiment to heal the gout and sciatica; as also joint-aches and other cold griefs. The very bearing of it about one eases the pains of the gout and defends him that bears it from the disease".

Historically used as a cure for gout, aches and pains, sciatica and inflammation, Ground Elder's use in herbal medicine has not changed much. Grieve wrote: "The roots and leaves boiled together, applied to the hip, and occasionally renewed, have a wonderful effect in some cases of sciatica." Roy Vickery has recommended an infusion of Ground Elder drunk twice a day for gout, and Le Strange noted that a leaf poultice can relieve rheumatic conditions or swollen joints.

James Duke, in his *Handbook of Medicinal Herbs* (2002), listed Ground Elder as a treatment for gout, sciatica, rheumatism, haemorrhoids, inflammation, and water retention. As a sedative, he recommended it for the relief of insomnia, as do other sources. Couplan described the plant's properties as stimulating, vulnerary and diuretic, while Le Strange wrote that a tea made from the leaves and root can be drunk as a diuretic (to increase urination). As in Gerard's time, the herb may be applied topically to reduce redness of the skin.

Though not the most popular herb in a herbalist's repertoire, Duke added certain cancers and tumours to the list of conditions that can be treated by Ground Elder. Keep in mind that any serious medical condition should be treated first by your doctor and that their advice should be sought before taking any herbal supplement.

SAFETY NOTE

Few side effects are noted either from eating Ground Elder or using it as a medicinal plant.

BOTANICAL PROFILE

Scientific Name: *Aegopodium podagraria.*

Family: Apiaceae.

Botanical Description

Height: 30 cms to 90 cms. Flowers: small flowers in numerous umbels, or clusters, turning from light-pink to white as they mature. Stems: erect, round, furrowed and hollow. Fruit/seeds: flat seed vessels developing from mature flower heads; wind pollinated. Leaves: large, long, hairless leaves in groups of three at the end of leaf stems; oval-shaped and finely toothed. Roots: a creeping root stock that spreads rapidly; planting buckwheat may drive out ground elder.

Flowers: May to July.

Status: Perennial. Not Native.

Habitat: Cultivated land, grassland, hedgerows, river banks, roadsides, scrub, wasteland.

Ground Elder (*Aegopodium podagraria*)

7
GROUND IVY

Mrs Grieve's essential reference *A Modern Herbal* tells us that Ground Ivy is one of Britain's commonest plants. It flourishes from sunny banks to shady wastelands. A perennial plant with trailing, dark-green, kidney-shaped leaves that retain their colour year-round, it has bluish flowers with a purple tint that can be seen in summer and autumn. Grieve noted that "its popular name is attributed to the resemblance borne by its foliage to that of the true ivy."

As she suggests, the plant's common name is misleading because it is not, in fact, a true ivy. However, the plant has a plethora of other names from which to choose: 'Gill-go-by-the-ground', 'Lizzy-run-up-the-hedge', 'cat's foot', 'devil's candlesticks' and 'alehoof' among others.

FOOD

Past and present literature on medicinal plants pays much attention to the volatile oils produced in glands beneath the leaves of

Ground Ivy. The oils lend the plant its distinctive balsamic odour and aromatic bitterness, once valued for improving the quality of beer and ale. The Saxons used Ground Ivy to enhance the flavour of beer and to clarify the brew. It was used in breweries for this reason up until the time of Henry VIII.

The plant's popularity in the sixteenth century, before the introduction of hops, led to common names such as 'alehoof', 'tunhoof' and 'gill-go-by-the-ground' from the French *'guiller'*, meaning 'to ferment'. Alehouses were sometimes known as gill houses, and the stakes outside the premises were entwined with Ground Ivy leaves. Gill also meant 'girl', and so Ground Ivy acquired the name 'hedgemaids'.

Gerard wrote that women of northern parts of Britain, and particularly in Wales and Cheshire, added Ground Ivy to ale to drive away "rheumatic humour flowing from the brain". The custom disappeared only a century later with the arrival of hops, according to British herbalist John Ray of Black Notley in Essex, though he acknowledged Ground Ivy could clear the head within a day. It's unlikely ale enriched with Ground Ivy was drunk purely for medicinal purposes; nevertheless its expectorant action was widely hailed as being good for coughs, colds and respiratory problems.

Culpeper (1653) wrote of alehoof, "It is good to tun up with new drink, for it will clarify it in a night, that it will be fitter to be dranke the next morning; or if any drinke be thick with removing or any other accident, it will do the like in a few hours."

For teetotallers, the country beverage 'gill tea' might have been preferable. It was made by steeping the plant in boiling water, sweetened with sugar, honey or liquorice, and was drunk after it had cooled. Tea is often purported to be medicinal, and gill tea was recommended for soothing coughs.

Ground Ivy tea was sold as a herb by the 'criers' in London markets, with claims it could purify the blood and stimulate digestion. In North America it was also used to make tea.

In Ludlow in Shropshire, England, Ground Ivy was called 'Robin-run-in-the-hedge' and served at Easter stuffed in a leg of pork. Its aromatic flavour made the leaves and stems a good substitute for mint or thyme in recipes for soups and egg and minced meat dishes, or they could be served as a 'mint' sauce on lamb. The juices of the leaves and stems could also be used in sauces for a variety of savoury dishes. The young shoots and leaves were eaten as greens like spinach, or made into soups, or added to raw salads. The uses of Ground Ivy in the kitchen seems limited only by the cook's imagination. It may be added to spice up salads, to flavour stews or omelettes, or as an addition to sandwich spreads. The leaves can be crystallised in the same way flowers are using lightly beaten egg white and caster sugar.

RECIPES

Ground Ivy and Horseradish Mayonnaise

- 15g fresh ground ivy leaves and stems
- 1 egg (can we take free-range as a given please)
- 200 ml rapeseed oil
- 3 tsp grated horseradish root
- 2 tbsp lemon juice

Add egg to a hand blender jug, along with 150ml of oil and lemon juice. Blitz until thick, if to thin add more oil. Add chopped ground ivy and horseradish root, then blitz until blended into the mayo.

Ground Ivy Tempura

- 2 handfuls of Ground Ivy leaves
- 150g plain flour
- 1 tbsp of cornflour
- 1 egg
- 300ml of cold water
- 100g rapeseed oil
- Soya sauce and/or honey
- Salt

Separate out the Ground Ivy leaves. In a chilled bowl, mix together the plain flour and cornflour, egg and cold water and a pinch of salt until you have a thin batter. Heat the oil until it is very hot. Dip each ground ivy leaf in the batter, until it is well coated, then fry the battered Ground Ivy leaves until lightly crisped, remove and drain on kitchen paper. Serve with soya sauce or honey

Tofu Marinated In Ground Ivy

- 7g ground ivy (fresh)
- 2tbsp olive oil
- 2tbsp sesame oil
- 1tbsp white wine vinegar
- 250g tofu

Finely chop the ground ivy, and combine all ingredients in a flat dish. Slice the tofu into four, and liberally brush the marinade all over it. Leave to stand for 30 minutes, turning the tofu occasionally. Next put ½ cup of oil in a frying pan on a high heat, when hot fry the tofu slices for 60 seconds either side. Serve on a bed of fried Dulse and serve topped with steamed or sautéed sea purslane leaves.

MEDICINE

Like many of our commonest plants, Ground Ivy was widely employed in folk medicine and attributed a wide range of actions such as diuretic, astringent and stimulating; and, of course, it was used as a health-giving tonic. Its impressive properties are described in ancient texts, from first-century Dioscorides and third-century Galen to sixteenth-century Gerard and seventeenth-century Culpeper. Gerard, for instance, wrote about Dioscorides' potion of Ground Ivy leaves for curing aching bones and sciatica, but noted that Galen attributed the plant's healing properties to its flowers. Culpeper added to Gerard's description of the "singular herb", suggesting that it could heal internal wounds, ulcerated lungs, stomach pains, problems of the spleen, gall and liver, and external wounds, gout, sores and ulcers. Among the more incredible claims in ancient texts, classical sage Hollerius is quoted: "The juice of this herb has cured many at the point of death, being drunk".

A principal use of the plant in folk medicine was for headaches, congestion, coughs and colds. It was even "extolled before all other vegetable medicines for the cure of consumption," said Grieve. The plant was gathered in spring to store and to make infusions for relieving colds throughout the year; a practice which continued in England up until the 1930s.

In the Scottish Highlands a snuff was made from the dried leaves to alleviate headaches. In fact, sniffing Ground Ivy juice was said to relieve headaches when all else had failed.

An infusion of Ground Ivy or the expressed juice was renowned in plant lore for eye problems, from sore or weak eyes to bruised and black eyes. The treatment involved simply washing the affected area. The Physicians of Myddfai in Wales used it to treat eye inflammations, as well as fevers and snake bites. Its fame as an eye medicine dates at least as far back as Saxon times, when the plant was boiled in sour beer to make an eye wash.

In Britain there are local accounts of Ground Ivy's use as an eye ointment (Dorset) and as an eye bath (Warwickshire). There is even a story of a fighting cock that got an eye wound during a fight and was cured after its owner chewed Ground Ivy leaves and spat in its eye.

A mother's tale from Shipston-on-Stour, Warwickshire, in September 1993, describes her son's eyes being sore as a result of gun smoke during army service. The woman sent her husband to the village gypsy, who prepared a decoction of Ground Ivy. This was said to clear up her son's troubles completely.

Ground Ivy was considered a powerful purifier, and was used by painters of the past to treat 'painter's colic', a condition caused by the lead in their paints. The remedy was a tea, drunk to relieve the bellyache of lead poisoning. In North America it was used by herbalists to treat poisoning from other heavy metals, such as mercury.

The plant's versatility in treating both major and minor complaints no doubt led to its widespread use as a home remedy. Any herb that could treat diarrhoea, tuberculosis, sinusitis, and 'glue ear' in children, and which could be used cosmetically for spots, pimples and sunburn, deserved a place in the herbalist's medicine cabinet.

An account by Lady Wilde in the 1800s described its use for epilepsy in Irish herbal medicine. It was mixed with mandrake (not an Irish plant) to make a plaster, and applied to the head. "If the patient sleeps he will do well, and if not, he will not".

By the nineteenth and twentieth centuries, modern herbalists were still using Ground Ivy to treat kidney problems, indigestion, cancer, ulcers, abscesses, and eye ailments. In Britain it retained its use as a herbal remedy for clearing catarrh and easing indigestion.

As recently as the late twentieth century in Ireland, Ground Ivy was used in herbal preparations for bronchitis, asthma, epilepsy, skin complaints, kidney blockages, to stimulate menstruation, as a diuretic, and to heal sores and blisters.

In today's herbals it may be listed for its anti-inflammatory, anti-viral, anticatarrhal, astringent and expectorant properties. It's still recommended for ear congestion caused by a cold, for ear blockages due to a build up of wax, and as being helpful for tinnitus.

Some research into Ground Ivy's chemistry can explain its medical history, in particular its component of ursolic acid, although this is a constituent present in many plants including apples, bilberries, cranberries, elder flower, peppermint, lavender, oregano, thyme, hawthorn, prunes. It is considered to be both anti-inflammatory and cytotoxic (harmful to cells). A study by Tokuda's group in 1986 found that Ground Ivy's ursolic acid could inhibit the Epstein Barr virus in mouse skin. The test prohibited tumour growth..

Let's remember that many medicinal plants have the potential to be poisonous before taking a look at the toxicity data for Ground Ivy. Its plant lore is rooted in witchcraft and it was drunk in alehouses for centuries – and most likely not always in moderation. It could cure a headache and remedy all manner of ills, yet cattle avoided it and grazing horses were said to come to harm because of it. It is still listed in today's herbals, but not considered a 'mainstream' herb like, for example, yarrow, nettle or rosehip. The story of Ground Ivy weaves a tight trail through our folk history, but it has not yet secured a place in most people's natural medicine cabinet.

SAFETY NOTE

Toxicity data for ursolic acid in the volatile oil of Ground Ivy – the constituent that makes the plant potentially helpful or harmful – is reportedly lacking. Some pharmacological findings are documented that support its use in herbal medicine, including that it "demonstrates cytotoxic activity against lymphocytic leukaemia, human lung carcinoma, and marginal activity against human colon and mammary tumors". However, the plant's safety during pregnancy is not confirmed and some suggest it may cause abortion.

It's recommended that those suffering from kidney disease should avoid it, because the plant's compounds might irritate the kidneys and gastrointestinal tract, and possibly harm the liver in large quantities. It's contraindicated in those who suffer with epilepsy, although some sources suggest there is nothing to support this.

BOTANICAL PROFILE

Scientific Name: *Glechoma hederacea*

Family: Lamiaceae

Botanical Description

Height: 0.2–1m; low-growing prostrate plant. Flowers: bluish, purplish flowers with four-sided stems. Leaves: trailing-evergreen, kidney-shaped leaves that resemble true ivy. Root: creeping root structure that deters other plants growing closely.

Flowers: March to June.

Status: Perennial. Native.

Habitat: Deciduous woodland, grassland, hedgerows, wasteland.

Ground Ivy (*Glechoma hederacea*)

8
PLANTAIN

Plantain belongs to a big family of around two hundred species in the plant group Plantaginaceae. Of these, twenty-five to thirty species have had a medicinal, culinary or other domestic use in our history and culture. Here, we focus mainly on the greater and lesser plantains known also as common plantain (*Plantago major*) and ribwort plantain (*Plantago lanceolata*) respectively. On occasion, other species may share the spotlight.

Plantain flourishes in different habitats around the world. In America and New Zealand it was called 'Englishman's foot' or 'white man's foot', because it followed British settlers as they colonised new land. Watts wrote that this legend more aptly describes "the persistent way that Great Plantain follows the tracks of man". The Latin name *'Plantago'* means 'sole of the foot', referring to the shape of the leaves rather than the plant's tendency to follow in human footsteps.

The species took advantage of agricultural practice in Britain, Ireland and Europe, with pollen samples found at archeological sites dating back some three to four thousand years. James Duke

(2000) tells us, "Its seeds long served as food, having been found in the stomachs of mummified 'bog people' of fourth century northern Europe."

Angela Paine (2006) described plantain as a "perennial opportunist" because of its survivalist nature. She wrote: "When growing in long grass it sends its leaves upwards, and competes with the grass for the light. When it grows in pastures grazed by animals it flattens itself to avoid being eaten." Plantain is disliked by gardeners, because it destroys grass with its vigorous rosette of leaves. Ribwort plantain is even less popular with hayfever sufferers, because of its highly irritant pollen.

FOOD

Grieve (1931) described the leaves as "bitterish and acrid to the taste; the root is saline and sweetish". Nevertheless, the plant earned a place in the list of forty-four salad herbs written by Scottish horticulturist John Abercrombie in his *Every Man His Own Gardener* (1787). Opinions vary. James Duke in his *Handbook of Edible Weeds* (2000) doesn't mince his words: "Except for its abundance and ease of recognition, I would have excluded this potherb, mainly because I don't like it. But then, I don't like spinach either. I've sampled all the plantain species I encountered around home and enjoyed none. Still, I would prefer plantain to starvation."

Mabey (1978) wrote that the raw leaves are tough and bitter, and better cooked like spinach as a side vegetable; he's unlikely to persuade Duke. François Couplan (1998) prefers the young leaves of greater plantain and ribwort plantain for their slightly bitter, mushroom-like flavour that works well in salads. He reserves the older leaves for making soups and vegetable dishes. He has recommended sautéing them in butter. The tiny flowers of the plant can be eaten raw – perhaps sprinkled on salads – or cooked.

Around the world, plantain has been collected as a salad green, vegetable and potherb, or for its seeds. It was a potherb in Ireland, but the leaves were also added to salads and the seeds were ground to make flour.

In the Mediterranean, greater plantain and ribwort plantain were enjoyed as a vegetable. The youngest leaves were picked in spring for salads, mixed with other wild vegetables, or made into soups. The plant was an ingredient in traditional Italian dishes *acquacotta* and *pistic*. In north-eastern Spain, plantain leaves were an ingredient in a traditional liqueur called *'ratafia'*. In south-west Spain and northern Italy, the flowering tops of greater plantain were used in a soup with a fungus flavour. In Turkey, ribwort plantain leaves were used to stuff vegetable pies.

In Lesotho, South Africa, the leaves and roots of greater plantain are eaten. In Australia, the seeds were eaten by early settlers in a starchy pudding similar to sago. A type of porridge is made by the Aborigine from a variety called 'shade plantain'.

In Nepal, ribwort leaves are cooked as a vegetable, and in the Himalayas, it's cooked in diluted milk. In China, plantain leaves were used as a potherb or eaten as a healthy spring green. The young plants were mixed with pork and used as a filling for a Chinese dumpling called *'jiao-zi'* in north-eastern territories. A similar species, *P. asiatica*, grew in damp regions and was sometimes sold with *P. major* at Chinese markets.

Various species of plantain have been collected as a wild edible over the centuries. In the sixteenth to nineteenth centuries, Buck's-horn Plantain, *Plantago coronopus* was grown in European herb gardens as a crispy salad leaf. In Italy, buckshorn is an ingredient in a traditional herb salad called *'misticanze'*. Sea Plantain, *Plantago maritima* has been gathered along the coasts of North America as a salad herb, to cook or to pickle. According to Thomas Elias and

Peter Dykeman (2009), Sea Plantain "is one of the best". The seeds of plantain have been used in Europe and Asia as a stabiliser for chocolate and ice cream.

As a wild edible, plantain species are considered highly nutritious, containing vitamins A, B, C and K, as well as calcium, fibre, fat, protein, silicon, sodium, zinc, tannin and mucilage. The nutty-flavoured seeds are also a good source of protein.

A study in 2001 by José Guil-Guerrero on the nutritional content of three plantain species – Greater Plantain (*P. major*), Ribwort Plantain (*P. lanceolata*) and Hoary Plantain (*P. media*) – found the plants were a potential source of food. He weighed up the nutrient value of plantains against their toxicity – that is, their nitrates, oxalic acids and saponins. He found the benefits of eating plantain outweighed its possible toxicity. Greater Plantain, in particular, was found to contain 45 mg of vitamin C per 100 g, leading the author to conclude "a minimum diet of 133 g of the fresh leaves of this species per day would provide a sufficient amount of vitamin C to meet the recommended daily allowance of 60 mg per person".

While plantain is currently not a commercial food source, ribwort is listed by the Council of Europe as a food flavouring. The US Food and Drug Administration lists plantain as a 'herb of undefined safety'. In Wiersema's and León's *World Economic Plants* (2013), several species of plantain are cited: *P. depressa, P. lanceolata, P. major, P. media, P. ovata, P. rugelii, P. arenaria,* and *P. virginica*.

Ribwort Plantain has had potential use as a fodder plant and as a fibre for manufacturing, but it has not been commercially cultivated. As a fodder for livestock, the plant is appreciated by sheep, goats and pigs, but disliked by cows and horses. Grieve wrote that the seeds are much loved by little birds and were collected near London to feed caged birds.

RECIPES

Aubergine and Avocado Bake With Ribwort Plantain

- 6 handfuls of young plantain leaves (ripped up)
- 3 aubergine (4mm slices)
- 1 onion (sliced)
- 4 garlic cloves (sliced)
- 1 avocado (halved and sliced)
- 400g greek strained yoghurt
- 400g passata (crushed tomatoes)
- rapeseed oil
- grated cheddar cheese
- cracked black pepper

Boil the ribwort plantain for 3 minutes, strain and squeeze the water out, then chop finely. Set aside. Blanch the aubergine in salted water, strain and set aside. Fry onion and garlic until soft, then add the ribwort plantain leaves, stir for 30 seconds, then add the passata. Cook until a thick sauce, and season with cracked black pepper.

Next put a layer of sliced aubergine in an ovenproof dish, then on top put the sliced avocado. Pour over half the ribwort plantain sauce, then smear with the greek yoghurt. Now add the remaining aubergine slices, and top with the remaining sauce and finish off with some grated cheese. Bake at 350°F/180°C/160 Fan for about 30 minutes or until it looks done.

Plantain Risotto

- 6 handfuls of arborio risotto rice
- 1 onion (chopped finely)
- 2 cloves of garlic (chopped)

- 150g Plantain (chopped)
- 2tbs dried dill
- 750ml stock
- 2 glugs of white wine
- 100g butter
- Cracked black pepper

Melt the butter and fry the onion with the garlic until the onion is translucent. Add the rice and stir so the grains are coated in butter. Now add a couple of glugs of white wine and allow the alcohol to evaporate. Keep stirring all the time.

Add dried dill, and mix in, add a ladle of hot stock, and keep stirring the rice mixture until the liquid is absorbed. Then add a second ladle and stir until the liquid is absorbed. Keep ladling in stock and repeating this process until the rice is done (about 20 minutes). It should be al dente. About five minutes before the rice is ready, add your chopped Plantain. The risotto needs to be gloopy but not soupy. Season with black pepper, and serve.

Spiced Plantain Seed Mix

- 1 handful of plantain seeds (either greater or ribwort)
- 3 handfuls of pumpkin seeds
- 3 handfuls of sesame seeds
- 1 tbsp tamari / soy sauce.

Put your seed mix into a non-stick frying pan and toast the seeds lightly. Add a tamari or soy sauce and coat the seed mix, allowing any excess sauce to evaporate. Turn out into bowls.

MEDICINE

In the first century, both Greek physician Dioscorides and Pliny the elder claimed plantain as a vulnerary herb that was good for healing sores and ulcers. In the third century, Greek physician Galen (129–c216 AD) praised plantain as an astringent and vulnerary herb.

The Celts made a drawing ointment from the medicinal plant which they used to heal wounds, and also made a curative lotion from plantain mixed with herbs such as honeysuckle, white roses and camphor. In the Scottish Highlands, plantain became known as 'slan-lus', the 'plant of healing'.

In the twelfth century, Hildegard of Bingen described plantain as a 'warm and dry' herb that could cure the effects of a love potion:

> "If a man or a woman
> eats or drinks a love potion,
> plantain juice should be
> given to them to drink."

To make a herbal medicine to apply to injuries and broken bones, Hildegard advised cooking the leaves or roots in water. The juice could be used to cure the sting of "a spider or some other vermin". Trotula, a healer and midwife of the twelfth century, said in her medical texts on women's health that plantain could treat uterine haemorrhages and even restore at least the appearance of a woman's virginity.

In the fifteenth century an ointment for wounds was made from a pint of ribwort juice mixed with a pint of vinegar and a pint of honey. Watts (2007) commented: "a pint of ribwort juice must have taken some collecting!" David Allen and Gabrielle Hatfield (2004) suggest a simpler remedy was to chew the leaves of Greater Plantain or Ribwort Plantain to release "healing chemicals" for treating wounds.

The sixteenth-century German botanist Hieronymus Bock claimed that the different species of plantain were among the best healing herbs for curing many conditions.

In the seventeenth century, physician and astrologer Nicholas Culpeper (1653) wrote it "cures the head by antipathy to Mars, neither is there hardly a martial disease but it cures." In early literature, plantain was frequently referenced as a healer of wounds. Shakespeare wrote in *Love's Labour's Lost* and *Romeo and Juliet* that it treated broken shins, and in *Troilus and Cressida* that it "heals the reaper's wounds".

Geoffrey Grigson (1996) alluded to the hardy nature of plantain plants when he wrote: "You tread on them, you crush them, and they go on living." This quality led to the belief in the sympathetic magic of plantain, because a plant so resilient to harm must be powerful enough to cure all wounds, injuries and bleeding. Richard Mabey (1978) wrote: "[Plantain] is one of those plants that positively thrives on rough treatment. The more you walk on it or mow it the better it thrives." In acknowledgement of its power, some wore plantain as an amulet around their necks as a supposed cure for the King's Evil, or scrofula – a type of skin disease.

In Irish folk medicine, Ribwort Plantain was said to bring the dead to life. It was believed to be the plant that healed Christ's wounds after the crucifixion. In West Galway, it was said ribwort was laid on the wound in Christ's side caused by a Roman spear.

A wide variety of plantains grow in Ireland, with records going back for generations. It was an important plant in Irish folk medicine for treating cuts, sores and bruises, because it could be collected almost everywhere. Buck's-horn Plantain (*P. coronopus*) and Sea Plantain (*P. maritima*) grew in coastal regions, and Greater Plantain (*P. major*) and Ribwort Plantain (*P. lanceolata*) were abundant in fields, waste grounds, roadsides, lawns and gardens. Any species of the plant could be made into a poultice, or the leaf alone applied as a 'bandage' to wounds. Peter Wyse Jackson (2014) wrote: "Bruised leaves, while still moist with the sap, were applied to the wound to diminish pain, stop profuse bleeding and prevent festering." A record from the Aran Islands tells of a plantain leaf applied to a cut on a finger that healed in seven days; it's possible the cut would have healed itself in seven days with or without the 'plantain plaster'. Another remedy from the Aran Islands used plantain leaves, washed and soaked in hot water, to treat whitlows (sores) on the ends of the fingers.

In the British Isles, the healing herb was a common ingredient in folk remedies until recent times. An ointment recipe in Lady Northcote's *The Book of Herbs* (1903) mentions plantain mixed with southernwood, blackcurrant, elder, angelica and parsley as a treatment for burns or weeping wounds. Grieve noted that the recipe, made by a woman from Exeter, England, was "in much request" twenty years after her death. In Guernsey, plantain leaves were chopped and mixed with egg whites to sooth burns.

Roy Vickery's anecdotal tales (1995) include an account by a wife who treated her husband's wounds with plantain leaves:

> "[She] picked the leaves of a variety of this plant from her garden and told me it would stop bleeding in a few minutes. When her husband cut himself when shaving she always got the leaves for him to put on. He himself would go and get a cobweb and put it on, and she said 'Of course that would stop the bleeding too.' [Andreas, Isle of Man, May 1963; Manx Folklife Survey]."

As a vulnerary herb, Mrs Grieve considered plantain useful for external bleeding, but not as a preventative for internal bleeding. In *A Modern Herbal* (1931), she listed its medical properties as cooling, diuretic (increased urination), deobstruent (clears blockages from the body such as by opening ducts) and astringent. She wrote it was a useful folk remedy for inflamed skin conditions, ulcers, insect stings and fevers. In Somerset, England, it was said that Greater Plantain leaves eased a bee sting – after the bee had been tricked into stinging a person for rheumatism. The plant mucilages of Greater Plantain leaves were thought to bring rapid pain relief after a wasp sting or mosquito bite, said Watts.

Taken internally, plantain could treat kidney disorders, bowel complaints, piles or intestinal worms, and acted as a diuretic. Culpeper (1653) recommended it for ringworm and shingles, among other ailments. He wrote that the juice mixed with rose oil eased "the pains of the head proceeding from heat. The same also is profitably applied to all hot gouts in the hands and feet". A syrup made from the seeds could treat thrush in children.

In Irish folk medicine, where plantain was widely acknowledged as a wound-healer, the juice was used to cure coughs, lumps and swellings, pimples, corns and warts, and to treat liver complaints and jaundice. The Irish believed that plantain leaves could be used to draw out pus from wounds: one side of the leaf had a drawing action, and the other side of the leaf was used for healing. A more unusual remedy in Ireland was using Ribwort Plantain to treat hydrophobia, or a fear of water.

William Salmon's herbal (1710) gave copious uses for Greater Plantain, including treating the throat, glands and lungs, clearing obstructions of the liver and spleen, and relieving symptoms of epilepsy, dropsy, jaundice, gout, headaches and even madness.

With its sole-shaped leaves, Greater Plantain was appropriately nicknamed 'traveller's plant' by some, and *The Good Housewife's Handmaid* (1588) gives it as a remedy to relieve tired feet. A record from South Uist in the Scottish Outer Hebrides suggests ribwort leaves were also used to treat weary feet. Watts gave the same use for Greater Plantain, "putting the leaves under the foot, or inside the stocking".

Remedies are recorded as having been made from both Greater Plantain and Ribwort Plantain throughout history in British folk medicine, for treating a range of ills from rashes and nettle stings to varicose veins. Greater Plantain seeds with egg yolks and flour could be made into cake to stop vomiting. The roots were also a traditional remedy for toothache. Ribwort Plantain was used for infections of the lung and bladder, for intestinal worms and as a laxative. It was also used in a lotion for the eyes. Both plants were picked to be made into tinctures, poultices, ointments, washes, gargles and syrups.

Another major use for plantain was as a cure for animal bites and stings. An old herbal, read by Grieve, stated: "If a wood hound (mad dog) rend a man, take this wort, rub it fine and lay it on; then will the spot soon be whole." The Welsh Physicians of Myddfai in the twelfth century used Greater Plantain mixed with sheep's sorrel, egg whites, honey and lard to make an ointment for dog bites. The plant was one of nine sacred herbs recorded in the *Lacnunga* (an ancient collection of Anglo-Saxon prayers and medical texts) as an ingredient for a salve to treat 'flying venom'.

In North America, plantain was known as 'snakeweed' because of the belief it cured snakebites. An account in Dr Robinson's *New Family Herbal*, published around the late nineteenth century, tells of an Indian cure for rattlesnake bite using plantain, which was recognised by the Assembly of South Carolina. The Ojibwe tribe carried

Greater Plantain with them for emergency protection against snakebites. Its protective power was known to weasels, according to the French, who said the wily animals rolled in plantain for protection against viper's bites.

Greater Plantain had various uses among Native American Indian tribes. The Chippewa used the leaves to draw out splinters and mixed the plant with bear grease as a vulnerary poultice. The leaves were stored over winter by greasing and wrapping in leather. The Iroquois and the Shoshone applied fresh leaves to wounds and bruises; the Iroquois also used the plant for respiratory infections and the Meskawaki used it for fevers. For the Navajo, Greater Plantain was one of 'life's medicines', used for many ailments including digestive complaints, heartburn, venereal disease and loss of appetite. Other North American uses for the herb included: as a remedy for rashes caused by poison ivy; as a treatment for rheumatism and epilepsy; to be smoked as a treatment for asthma (which seems a contradiction); and spreading of the seeds on bread and butter to remedy worms in children.

In the Caribbean, the plant was used to treat eye inflammations. The leaves were also made into a herbal tea, with mint, thyme and salt, to treat shock or to promote menstrual bleeding.

In the Himalayas, the leaves were crushed and made into a paste that was applied to sore joints. The seed husks were mixed with sugar and water, and taken for constipation, internal inflammation and jaundice.

In traditional Chinese medicine, Greater Plantain is regarded as a remedy for dysentery, diarrhoea, urinary problems, hepatitis, and lung problems such as asthma and bronchitis.

In Russia, a decoction of Ribwort Plantain treated constipation, and an infusion of the seeds treated sterility.

While plantain was in widespread use around the world, the different species were often described indiscriminately in herbals. Grieve wrote that Buck's-horn Plantain had similar properties to Greater Plantain and Ribwort Plantain: "The qualities, specifications, preparation and virtues are the very same as those of *Plantago major*". Hoary Plantain (*P. media*), found throughout Europe, was also used as a substitute for Greater or Ribwort Plantain.

Richard le Strange, in his *A History of Herbal Plants (1977)*, wrote about four different species of plantain: Common (Greater) Plantain, Ribwort (Lesser) Plantain, Buck's-horn Plantain and Psyllium Plantain. He refers to sixteenth-century herbalist John Gerard's descriptions of the herbs: buck's-horn could cure "the stranguary" (a bladder blockage or irritation), stones in the body, shivering fevers, and sore eyes; psyllium could relieve swollen joints. Watts noted that Gerard placed Greater Plantain above the rest: "Of all the plantains the greatest is the best".

Around the world, Ispaghul Plantain (*P. ovata*) is found in countries such as the Canary Islands, Spain, Iran and India, and the seeds are used to treat diarrhoea, dysentery, and inflamed intestines.

In veterinary medicine, plantain treated ailments in cattle such as sore udders or bites. Jackson wrote that it was fed to dogs to stop them from going mad; the prevention of madness in either humans or animals appears to be a common theme.

The seed heads of Greater Plantain were once soaked for the gelatinous matter that was used as a starch for muslin.

Bartram's Encyclopedia of Herbal Medicine (2002) describes Greater Plantain as "one of the most versatile of herbal medicines", similar in action to Ribwort Plantain – but *"Plantago major* is preferred". Its medical properties are indicated for numerous conditions: blood disorders, neuralgia, kidney and bladder problems, bedwetting, irritable bowel syndrome, dysentery, bleeding piles, ulcers, blood in stools or urine, excessive menstrual bleeding, cystitis, thrush, lesions, skin diseases, bleeding gums, toothache, fevers, and diabetes.

Umberto Quattrocchi's *World Dictionary of Medicinal and Poisonous Plants* (2012) provides a greater number of ailments that may be treated by *P. major* but also includes medical uses for *P. lagocephala*, *P. lanceolata*, *P. macrocarpa*, *P. maritima*, *P. media*, *P. ovata*, *P. paralias*, and *P. patagonica*. Greater Plantain is the only species he mentions in relation to the practice of veterinary medicine, although Ribwort Plantain is preferred for bites and stings, and Hoary Plantain (*P. media*) as an insect repellant.

Overall, different species of plantain have similar uses in modern herbalism, although certain species are sometimes highlighted for specific use. Psyllium Plantain, for example, is said to be an excellent laxative. The mucilaginous seeds are soaked in water and swell up to provide a bulking agent for stools that is also soothing to mucous membranes.

All plantain leaves contain plant tannins that could support their use as a healing agent for cuts, grazes, bruises and wounds. The mucilage in the plant leaf is soothing to wounds and to intestinal irritations. The plant polysaccharides can stimulate the immune system and help fight off infection. The plant flavonoids too can strengthen the immune system and protect the liver. Plantain is also thought to lower cholesterol. Its use in the treatment of venomous bites and stings is extended to stopping the necrosis of a spider's bite.

Plantain's medical prowess has grown since the days of Dioscorides, Pliny and Galen – today's texts even list it in the treatment of breast cancer and colon cancer. Duke's *Handbook of Medic-*

inal Herbs (2002) lists seventeen different types of cancer that can be treated with Greater Plantain.

The seeds can be made into a tincture by soaking and straining in alcohol, or the leaves can be made into an infusion; either tincture or infusion make an ointment with beeswax and oil. A plantain tea might relieve symptoms of hayfever and asthma. Some evidence exists for its use in respiratory problems, Karalliedde and Gawarammana (2010) reported.

Recent research into the plant's chemistry has revealed many active compounds, including compounds that are anti-inflammatory, antibacterial and antiviral, as well as those which strengthen the immune system and fight tumours. Paine (2006) wrote: "The few clinical trials that have been carried out appear to vindicate the thousands of years of traditional use and suggest that plantain is a valuable herbal medicine." In a clinical trial to investigate the effects of plantain on patients suffering from gastroduodenitis found that the plant helped to improve their symptoms significantly, and may have stopped internal bleeding (Chakarski, 1982). Another study a year later demonstrated that plantain helped patients to recover from bronchitis (Koichev, 1983). The plant's antispasmodic properties have been used to treat chronic coughing (Wegener, 1999). More recent research has shown that plantain leaves may prevent ulcers from forming (Samuelsen, 2000).

Is there nothing plantain can't treat? Arthur Haines wrote in his *Ancestral Plants* (2010): "*Plantago major* and its close relatives provide very potent medicines for many types of ailments. The efficacy of this common plant never ceases to amaze me."

SAFETY NOTE

While plantain pollen can be an irritant to hayfever sufferers, the plant itself may sometimes cause allergic contact dermatitis. It's thought the green parts contain an irritant substance and that the seeds can cause dermatitis. Furthermore, Karalliedde and Gawarammana (2010) reported: "Allergy to *Psyllium* seeds has been reported in people who had no previous allergy and in those with a history of occupational exposure to plantain."

Excessive consumption of plantain might have an unwanted laxative effect and could lower blood pressure. Some sources suggest plantain should not be taken by patients using digitalis.

BOTANICAL PROFILE

Common Name: Greater Plantain.

Scientific Name *Plantago major.*

Family: Plantaginaceae.

Botanical Description

Height: 10–60 cm. Fruit: small seed-bearing capsule. Flowers: long, cylindrical spikes covered in tiny yellow-green flowers with yellow anthers. Leaves: long, ribbed, green leaves. Roots: short rootstock with long and fibrous roots.

Flowers: June to October.

Status: Perennial. Native.

Habitat: Cultivated land, roadsides, wasteland.

Common Name: Ribwort Plantain.

Scientific Name: *Plantago lanceolata.*

Family. Plantaginaceae.

Botanical Description

Height: 5–70 cm. Fruit: small seed-bearing capsule. Flowers: long stalks bear cylindrical, brownish flowering spikes with yellow anthers. Leaves: long and green, lance-shaped, ribbed leaves. Roots: short taproot with fibrous roots.

Flowers: April to October.

Status: Perennial. Native.

Habitat: Cultivated land, grassland, roadsides, wasteland.

Greater Plantain (*Plantago major*)

Ribwort Plantain (*Plantago lanceolata*)

9
PRIMROSE

The Primrose is one of the first spring flowers you may notice in your garden. In the language of flowers, it means 'youth', although in the fickleness of youth the Primrose says, "Maybe I will love you. I cannot say yet". The popularity of its bright yellow blossoms have made the flower scarce in London and other cities where it has been picked, according to Geoffrey Grigson (1996), perhaps more than any other wildflower except the bluebell. Its decline is also due to changes in woodland management and the loss of the shaded habitat so favoured by the plant.

In medieval Latin, Primrose, or prima rosa, meant 'first rose' of the year. In early literature, there is a lack of distinction between *P. vulgaris* and the common cowslip (*P. veris*). The two plants are often referred to interchangeably, or as one and the same, in folklore and customs. Even in today's herbals, Primroses and cowslips are frequently listed as the same entry; for instance, Richard le Strange's *A History of Herbal Plants* describes the attributes of cowslips, Primroses and auriculas under a general heading of 'Primula'.

FOOD

Sixteenth-century Flemish herbalist Rembert Dodoens may not have found a use for Primroses in his medicine cabinet, but he wrote that cowslips were eaten with other vegetables in many countries and in a variety of dishes including purees, pies, omelettes and pancakes. The English Primrose that grows so neatly along the borders of flower beds was once popular in England as a primula stew or pottage. Jackson (2014) wrote: "The flowers may also be fermented to make wine or ground with rice, almonds, honey and saffron to make a 'Primrose pottage'". The leaves could be boiled as a green vegetable. Both the fresh flowers and the leaves were used in salads or to make the well-known English Primrose tea.

Hatfield tells us that delicate Primrose flowers were made into wine by our ancestors, although she feels "they certainly couldn't be gathered in sufficient quantity today". However, Sturtevant's *Edible Plants of the World* (1972) suggests that Primrose wine remains a popular drink in some parts. "The flowers are picked when first open and fermented with water and sugar. The liquor, when well prepared, is pleasant in flavor and very intoxicating, resembling in taste some of the sweet wines of the south of France. In many parts of England, Primrose flowers are collected in large quantities for this purpose".

Today's edible uses for the plant are similar to those of the past. The mildly sweet-scented flowers may be eaten raw in salads – either vegetable salads or fruit salads – or cooked as a vegetable. They may be used in conserves, custards, mousse, tarts or other desserts and confections. In fact, the flowers make an attractive garnish to any dish. Richard Mabey (1978) suggested strewing them on roast meats or eating them candied.

The leaves make an alternative salad green and have a reportedly spicy taste with a slight anise aroma. They can be cooked in the pot, added to soup, or mixed with other herbs as a stuffing for meat or poultry. Both blooms and leaves can be made into syrup or tea, the latter being renowned for its soothing qualities.

Nutritionally, the leaves contain vitamin C and minerals. François Couplan (1998) wrote that the whole plant, particularly the root, contains saponins, glucosides, and various other substances. Sulejman Redžić's 2006 paper on wild edible plants in Bosnia and Herzegovina reports that *P. vulgaris* leaves contain over 300 mg of vitamin C per 100 g.

RECIPES

Candied Primrose

- 25 primrose flowers
- 1 egg white
- 1 tsp cold water
- 50g icing sugar

Gather the primroses on a dry day. Separate the flowers from the calyx. Make an egg wash by beating the egg white with cold water. Using a new paintbrush just for food, paint the egg wash on each flower both front and back. Pour the icing sugar into a bowl. Place the flower in the sugar and coat as much as possible. Take out and place on a tray that is covered with greaseproof paper and leave to dry until they have hardened. This might take 1 to 2 days or maybe a bit longer. Store in a tissue lined Tupperware box.

Warm Primrose Salad

- Primrose shoots

- Sea salt
- Water

Soak the primrose shoots in salt water for 30 minutes. Then bring a pot of water to the boil and simmer the shoots for 5 minutes. Drain and serve with a vinaigrette dressing of your choice.

Primrose Tart

- 1 handful of fresh Primrose flowers
- 1 egg yolk
- Mace (a pinch)
- 2 tbs butter (melted)
- 100g ricotta cheese
- Ready bought tart cases

Place Primrose flowers in a pan and add enough water to just cover them. Boil the flowers for about 5 minutes until they are soft. Using a slotted spoon, scoop them out and put in a bowl. Pound the flowers until you have a paste then add the ricotta cheese, butter, mace and egg yolk. Mix all the ingredients well, then spoon into your tart cases. Bake in an over at 350°F/180°C/160 Fan for about 20 minutes until golden brown. Keep checking to make sure they don't burn.

MEDICINE

As a magical plant, Primroses were believed to be helpful for all manner of ailments. Three Primroses were swallowed to cure a fever in Denmark and Germany, or to treat a swollen neck in Romania. The flower was also a remedy for melancholy, as recommended by Hildegard of Bingen, who in the twelfth century wrote:

> "When melancholy rises up in a person, it makes the person sad and turbulent in his or her moods … Let the person place this herb on the flesh, near the heart, until it warms them up. The airy spirits who wear the person out will cease to torment them because they dread the strength that this herb takes from the sun."

Some suggest that for this reason, the Primrose was associated with melancholy, rather than youth, in the language of flowers, although the two might be said to go hand in hand.

The Primrose was often linked to people's health and wellbeing in England. For instance, when the population of a village in Suffolk was decimated by plague, it was said that all the Primroses died and would no longer grow there. In Cheshire, a Primrose blossoming in winter was an omen of death. In the Lake District, a single Primrose brought into the house was a sign of death in the family.

From magic to medicine, however, "it is no easy matter to find out whether Primroses were used for medicinal purposes in Antiquity," wrote de Cleene and Lejeune. Either the plant appears under a different name, such as cowslip, or its description does not match our present-day identification of *Primula vulgaris*. Thus, it's easy to see where the confusion lies. De Cleene and Lejeune tell us that cowslips were not found in Greece and that the species is not mentioned in classical manuscripts, while Pliny's description "does not remind us of a Primrose". Nevertheless, the flower does appear in the manuscripts of the ancient Physicians of Myddfai in Wales, who wrote: "whosoever shall have lost his reason or his speech, let him drink of the juice of the Primrose, within two months afterwards, and he will indeed recover".

The flower gradually found its way into medieval herbals, but it was often mentioned as cowslip or alongside use with other herbs. Rembert Dodoens (1517–1585) wrote: "The Primrose is used in combination with other herbs in food / but in medicine it has no power worth mentioning" (quoted in de Cleene and Claire Lejeune, 2003). William Turner wrote in his herbal (1568): "The flowers of cowslips conserved in sugar and also the stilled water thereof are very good for them that are weak and very low brought by long sickness, and it has a singular property to comfort the heart." John Gerard (1597) wrote about the Primrose as a remedy for 'phrensie', referring to a type of delirium or feverish madness, and for migraine. "Primrose Tea," said Gerard, "drunk in the month of May is famous for curing the phrensie." The juice of the plant was also drunk in Wales as a treatment for madness, while a decoction of the leaves was thought to cure forgetfulness. Gerard also recommended the flowers soaked in vinegar to cure the King's Evil (scrofula) and ailments of the throat.

Over the years, the flower did find a place in the medicinal garden. Indeed, by the days of Nicholas Culpeper (1653) Primroses were, of course, "so well known, that they need no description". He recommended the leaves as a salve to heal wounds, but strongly emphasised the healing power of the flowers:

> "The flowers are held to be more effectual than the leaves, and the roots of little use. An ointment being made with them, takes away spots and wrinkles of the skin, sunburning, and freckles, and adds beauty exceedingly; they remedy all infirmities of the head … false apparitions, phrensies, falling sickness, palsies, convulsions, cramps, pain in the nerves … the flowers take away trembling … Because they strengthen the brain and nerves … and Greeks gave them the name Paralysis".

Despite the roots being of 'little use', Culpeper suggested they were "used as a sternutory to the head" to induce sneezing. He added that the roots might ease pains in the back and bladder as well.

The Primrose's reputation for healing wounds endured for many centuries. Woodmen of Hampshire and the New Forest, in England, treated their injuries with a 'cut ointment' made from Primroses boiled in lard.

In Irish folk medicine, Primroses were also used as an ointment for burns, cuts and skin ailments. Peter Wyse Jackson (2014) tells us: "In Co. Kildare the leaves were made into an ointment and rubbed on piles and in Co. Kerry they were rubbed on the face to cure razor cuts ... in Co. Westmeath the flowers were made into a paste with pig fat to treat burns."

Indeed, the plant had many uses in Irish folk medicine. The leaves were valued as a remedy for toothache (being rubbed on the tooth) as well as to treat jaundice, stomach pains and insomnia. In Kildare, boiled Primroses were a cure for tuberculosis.

Their use varied across Britain also. In Suffolk, England, the leaves were dried and soaked in linseed oil to apply to burns. People in Suffolk also used a healing ointment of Primroses in pork lard to treat ringworm. A tea of Primroses was drunk to treat coughs and colds. An infusion of the flowers was a remedy for sore throats. The juice of the leaves was mixed with gin to prevent strokes. According to Mrs Grieve's *A Modern Herbal* (1931), Primrose was an important remedy for rheumatism and gout and the raw leaves were eaten to cure arthritis.

By the nineteenth century in North America, Primrose was used in folk medicine to treat paralysis – just as the ancients had recommended – as well as rheumatism and gouty conditions – just as was recommended in early herbalism.

Hatfield noted that Primrose was recognised as a great 'soother' in folk medicine. The flowers made healing salves for skin conditions and burns, and the infused leaves made a soothing eyewash. In

Dorset, an ointment made from Primroses and bramble tips was used for getting rid of pimples. In Ireland, the juice of Primroses was used to remove wrinkles. A gypsy cure for skin complaints involved drinking water infused with three Primrose leaves. A record from the Outer Hebrides suggests Primrose leaves were applied to cure persistent boils on the legs.

In Irish veterinary folk medicine, Primrose roots crushed in breast milk were once used to treat coughs in horses.

The Primrose (*Primula vulgaris*) has had three main uses in folk medicine that particularly stand out, according to Allen and Hatfield (2004): as an ointment for wounds, a treatment for skin complaints, and as a relaxant. While Hatfield (2007) mentions that the herb is little used in modern practice, a preparation is still sometimes used as a mild laxative and diuretic (to increase urination). The diuretic effects are thought to be due to the plant's saponins which make it a helpful herb for rheumatism and gout. In Italy, for example, Primrose (*P. vulgaris*) is among the wild food plants noted to have beneficial effects due to its diuretic properties, as well as being valued for its sedative and antispasmodic actions.

Several herbal texts list the plant's medical properties as antispasmodic, anthelmintic (destroying parasitical intestinal worms), astringent, and anti-inflammatory. A tincture or ointment of the plant might yet prove useful for healing minor ulcers and wounds.

While Culpeper favoured the flower, Grieve valued both the root and flower. She wrote in 1931:

> "Both the root and flowers of the Primrose contain a fragrant oil and Primulin, which is identical with Mannite, whilst the somewhat acrid active principle is Saponin."

The saponins also contribute an expectorant effect and might support the plant's use as a remedy for coughs and colds. In addition, Primrose contains salicylates, which are a main ingredient of aspirin and which may support its use as an anti-inflammatory.

Grieve recommended a teaspoonful of powdered root as an emetic (to induce vomiting, perhaps to treat intestinal worms) and a tablespoonful to treat nervous headaches. One of the most popular uses for the plant remains as a sedative to treat restlessness and insomnia. Grieve tells us that Primrose is particularly used for this purpose in the US. An infusion of the roots is considered a good remedy against nervous headaches.

As a cosmetic, Primrose is a remedy for freckles. The flowers might also be made into a simple home-made salve when infused in lard, or another base such as beeswax, and applied as a healing ointment.

SAFETY NOTE

Couplan reports that the leaves of some exotic species of Primrose may cause dermatitis. *Herbalpedia* suggests that *P. vulgaris* should not be used by pregnant women, patients sensitive to aspirin, or those on anti-coagulant drugs such as warfarin.

BOTANICAL PROFILE

Scientific Name: *Primula vulgaris.*

Family: Primulaceae.

Botanical Description

Height: up to 10–25 cm. Flowers: large, yellow-green flowers appearing to grow out of a rosette. Leaves: lance-shaped, rosette of leaves tapering to the stalk. Root: knotty root stock with long, shaggy stalks rising up.

Flowers: March to May.

Status: Perennial. Native.

Habitat: Deciduous woodland, hedgerows, scrub.

Primrose (*Primula vulgaris*)

10

RAMSONS (WILD GARLIC)

Wild Garlic (*Allium ursinum*) is a plant of shady, damp woodlands, fields and hedgerows. Peter Wyse Jackson (2014) wrote that it is found growing throughout Britain, Ireland and Europe. Its tiny, white flowers and bright green leaves form a canopy beneath the trees in some places, while in other areas it's quite scarce. Mac Coitir (2015) remarked that the plant is commonplace in Irish woods, where it creates a flowering carpet of star-like, white blossoms in place of the often-seen flooring of blue bluebells.

The English naturalist William Turner knew the plant in 1548 as ramsey, bucrammes (buck rammes) and rammes. It is also known as 'ramson' or 'Ramsons', and several places in England share its name, such as Ramsbottom (meaning 'ramson valley') in Lancashire and Ramsey (meaning 'ramson island') in Essex and Huntingdonshire. The plant was a metaphor for bitterness in Irish folklore. There was a saying in County Donegal: "As bitter as Wild Garlic" (quoted in Mac Coitir).

Another of the plant's common names, that of 'bear garlic', comes from the belief that bears ate Wild Garlic to regain their strength after a long winter's slumber. *Ursinum* is Latin for 'bear'. *Herbalpedia* (2014) tells us: "Plants of the bear contain the power of renewal and purification. Specifically, they break up hardenings, warm the body and make a person 'as strong as a bear'." Bear garlic was well known to the ancient Romans, Celts and Teutonic tribes as one of the oldest healing plants.

FOOD

Wild Garlic is a less well-known table vegetable than its domesticated relative, but it can be used in the same way as any herb or green. Finely chop or bruise the plant to use raw in salads and sandwiches, or boil and mix with other vegetables to make into soups and side dishes.

Gerard (1597) praised its distinctive taste: "The leaves of Ramsons be stamped and eaten of divers in the Low-countries, with fish for a sauce, even as we do eate greene-sauce made with sorrel. The same leaves may very well be eaten in April and May with butter, of such as are of a strong constitution, and laboring men" (quoted in De Cleene and Lejeune, 2003).

The plant was an important wild edible in ancient Ireland. Jackson (2014) wrote:

> "Chopped leaves add interest to salads or can be added to flavour other foods, such as stews, sauces, soup or soft cheeses and cottage cheese. The leaves can also be made into a puree with nuts, mustard leaves, olive oil and lemon juice to make a pesto that can be used with pasta or added as flavouring to stews, burgers and other meats."

Mac Coitir tells us it was often gathered to eat raw or cooked in soup or broth. The leaves could be wrapped around lamb or fish and grilled for a mild garlic flavour, or chopped with butter and spread over French bread to make "Wild Garlic bread". As recently as the nineteenth century in Ireland, Wild Garlic was used to flavour butter instead of salt. It was also used to make bog butter: "Butter was wrapped in garlic and then buried in the bogs to flavour and preserve it" (Jackson, 2014). For a quick bite, the young leaves can be eaten with bread and butter, and the flowers can be sprinkled on salads.

The wild herb was so highly valued in Ireland that, according to the Old Irish Brehon laws, there was a fine for stealing it from private land – the poacher would forfeit "two and a half milch cows". One wonders how the penalty of two and a half cows was paid.

François Couplan wrote in his book *Le Régal Végétal* in 2009 that bear (wild) garlic has been one of the most widely consumed wild plants in Europe since human history began. It has been picked by individuals and families, sold in markets (including in France and Switzerland), and commercially marketed in the form of cheese, ravioli (*agnolotti*), sauces and condiments.

The food industry sources much of the plant from Eastern Europe. In Romania, the leaves of "garlic of the bears" are eaten in spring salads dressed with oil and vinegar, cooked like spinach, or made into a sour soup ('*ciorba*'); in Serbia and Bosnia, the leaves and bulbs are eaten ('*srijemoé*'); and in Poland, the leaves are fermented in lactic acid and called '*Kiszonyczosnekniedzwiedzi*'.

In Russia, Wild Garlic (*A. ursinum*) and a closely related species (*A. victorialis*) are used as an ingredient in a salad known as '*cheremsha*'.

If you can encourage Wild Garlic to grow on your doorstep, you will have the benefit of its highly nutritious leaf and bulb. The leaves per 100 g contain 45 mg of vitamin C and almost 5 mg of beta carotene. The bulbs per 100 g have 16 mg of vitamin C and over 2 mg of protein. The plant bulb is also a significant source of energy, with almost 16 g of carbohydrate per 100 g (Pieroni and Quave, 2014).

The plant has a strong garlic smell that might not appeal to everyone, but its mild flavour is more reminiscent of onions. Wild food forager Richard Mabey (1978) recommended substituting Wild Garlic for garlic or spring onion in salads or sauces, or chopping the leaves to flavour sour cream or mayonnaise. He added that the leaves compliment tomato and that "one Italian chef in the Chilterns (who also makes flavoured olive oil by soaking Ramsons leaves in it) sometimes adds them to tomato sauces instead of basil". As the wild edible is best picked in spring, making an infusion in olive oil is a good way to enjoy its subtle flavour and culinary benefits all year round; the leaves can also be frozen or made into a pesto sauce to enjoy later in the season. However, when dried, the herb loses much of its pungent taste.

Wild Garlic makes a fine addition to omelettes, cream cheeses, dips and sauces, and can be eaten as a side vegetable to fish. The bulbs, as well as leaves, can be chopped and cooked in casseroles, and the leaf bulbils can be used like capers. Adventurous cooks might want to explore 'Ramsons risotto', 'bear garlic soup', and 'beartsiki' – a twist on the Greek tsatsiki. Alternatively, Wild Garlic adds a simple twist to most meals. You can mix it with other vegetables, eat a handful with bread, add it to a salad or make a tasty garlicky butter or cottage cheese to spread on bread.

If you don't have time to make an elaborate meal, don't worry. Wild Garlic leaves are simply delicious in peanut butter sandwiches, according to late English ecologist Oliver Rackham (Mabey, 1978).

The juice of Ramsons was once used as a household disinfectant. The garlic-smelling leaves were used in Scotland to repel midges.

Other species of the garlic and onion (*Allium*) family can be used similarly to Ramsons, wrote Mabey: "These include three-cornered garlic (*Allium triquetrum*) quite commonly naturalised in the south-west, and wild onion or crow garlic (*Allium vineale*) common in arable fields and waysides".

RECIPES

Wild Garlic and Nettle Pesto

- 50g wild garlic leaves (shredded)
- 30g hairy bittercress rosettes
- 20g fresh young nettle tips
- 10g walnuts
- lemon juice (add to taste)
- organic rapeseed oil (add to taste)
- parmesan or a hard goats cheese (add to taste)

Put the wild garlic, nettles and hairy bittercress into a food processor and 'blitz' until roughly chopped. Next drizzle in the oil add the grated cheese and lemon juice, Use your senses to find out which amounts suit your palette. Serve with oat cakes or crudités, however I just spoon it into my mouth. Serves 4.

Wild Garlic Pakoras

- 250g gram flour (chickpea flour)
- 50g self-raising flour
- ½ tsp red chilli powder
- 1 tsp garam masala
- 1 tsp tandoori masala powder
- 1 lemon (juiced)

- 300g potatoes
- 1 onion, (finely chopped)
- 100g Wild Garlic leaves
- 1 green chilli
- 1 tsp salt
- 500ml of sunflower oil

Dice the potatoes small, then parboil until just done, and strain. Sift the gram and self-raising flour together into a bowl, then add the chilli powder, garam masala and tandoori masala powder, and mix in well. Now add the lemon juice, then enough water to make a smooth batter. It needs to be thick enough to coat the back of a spoon. Then set aside for 30 minutes.

Next blitz the Wild Garlic and green chilli in a food processor until it looks like chopped parsley. You can use a knife, but I am lazy. Then add this to the batter mix along with the potato and onion and stir in well so everything is coated with batter. Heat the sunflower oil in a saucepan. It's hot enough when you can drop a bit of the batter into it and it starts gently frying. Next, drop tablespoons of the batter mixture into the hot oil, and cook for 3 minutes, before turning over and cooking for a further 3 minutes. Take out of the pan and drain on kitchen paper. Serve when cool. Makes 16 pakoras.

Wild Garlic Kimchi

- 1kg of wild garlic leaves and stems
- 75g of course Korean red pepper powder known as gochugaru
- 3tbsp grated ginger
- 150g grated daikon (mooli)
- 1tbsp clearlight ume shiso/ume plum seasoning

- 2tbsp dried sea lettuce sprinkles
- 2tbsp sea salt

Wash the wild garlic leaves and stems. Shake dry and roughly chop. In a bowl combine and mix well the Korean red pepper, grated ginger, grated daikon, sea lettuce, sea salt and ume shiso. Add this paste to the chopped wild garlic leaves and using your hands, thoroughly squeeze and press the wild garlic until everything is covered with the paste and there is a decent amount of liquid coming from the mixture.

Next put into a clip-top Kilner jar. Press the mixture down, then close the lid. Allow to sit for a week before taste testing. Will keep for a few months (maybe longer) either in the refrigerator or not. Makes 1.5 litres

MEDICINE

Ancient Greek physician Dioscorides wrote in the first century that garlic could cure the bites of snakes, although this remedy was little mentioned in the works of early herbalists in Britain and Ireland. Early healers among the Celts, Teutonic tribes and ancient Romans were familiar with the wild herb and called it *'herba salutaris'*, meaning 'healing herb'.

The Physicians of Myddfai, a group of herbalists first recorded around the thirteenth century in Wales, used Wild Garlic as a healing plant. Its medicinal value was believed to be in its being diaphoretic (inducing sweating), diuretic (increasing urine flow), expectorant (easing breathing), stimulating, and antiseptic. A remedy was recorded by the Welsh physicians: "For a swelling of the stomach. Take goats' whey, and pound the herb called Ramsons, mixing together and straining. Let it be your only drink for three days".

John Gerard wrote that Wild Garlic was good for curing stones in the body. His recommendation was carried into the Scottish Highlands and Islands, where an infusion of the leaves was drunk for 'gravel' or 'stone'; the remedy was sometimes taken with brandy. The plant was made into a poultice for infected wounds and an infusion drunk as a blood tonic.

Wild Garlic was greatly valued in Irish folk medicine for its healing properties. It was eaten raw or boiled in milk and rubbed onto skin as a remedy; although it was considered most potent as simply a medicinal food. The herb was used to treat a host of illnesses: toothache, worms, warts, corns, sores (specifically on the fingers), blisters, wounds, sore eyes, toothache, coughs, colds, flu, sore throats, chest and lung infections, asthma, stomach aches, indigestion, kidney problems, measles, mumps, rheumatism, sciatica and tuberculosis; it was even used as a blood purifier and to dissolve blood clots. As a cure for rheumatism in Ireland, the leaves were boiled in water and added to a bath, or barrel, for the whole body to bathe in.

The vast range of diseases for which Wild Garlic was indicated in Ireland meant it was regarded as a panacea, wrote Gabrielle Hatfield. "'Nine diseases shiver before the garlic' is a [County] Sligo saying". The herb was carried in people's pockets to ward off flu during the 1918 pandemic in Ireland. In other parts of the British Isles, the leaves of Wild Garlic were worn under the soles of the feet, inside shoes or socks, to prevent people from catching coughs and colds.

On the Isle of Man, the bulbs were pickled in brown sugar and rum to be stored over winter as a cough and cold remedy. Roy Vickery has provided an account from the Manx Folklife Survey, October 1991:

"[Reminiscences of … licensee of the Halfway House, between Douglas and Peel, who died in 1973, aged 90]. In the 1930s the pub had a garden/orchard. *Allium ursinum* grew at one end of the orchard. Bulbs were dug when they first sprouted in spring, washed and dried in the sun on a clean tea towel. Then packed into a wide-mouthed glass jar with dark brown sugar. Light Jamaica rum was poured over and the whole was stored in a cool dark place – e.g. a wardrobe – until the following winter, when it was used for chesty coughs and colds."

Wild Garlic was considered a good preventative in Irish folk medicine to ward off coughs, colds and flu – a belief that was shared in other parts of Britain. A seventeenth-century proverb said eating leeks in March and Ramsons in May would keep the doctor away:

> Eat leeks in Lide [March] and ramsins in May
> And all the year after physitians may play.
>
> — *CN FRENCH, A COUNTRYMAN'S DAY BOOK (1929)*

In Ireland, Wild Garlic was sometimes employed as a veterinary remedy for various ailments in horses and cattle, such as ringworm in calves. In County Westmeath, the herb was grown in fields for cows to graze because of its beneficial effects; some complained that it tainted the flavour of the butter. As recently as 2001, there is a record of Wild Garlic cloves being used – inserted under the tail – to treat cattle diseases. Sometimes a mixture of garlic, soot and goose dung was applied and bandaged in position.

Wild Garlic (*A. ursinum*) has many benefits over its domesticated cousin (*A. sativum*). It was recognised as 'Plant of the Year' in 1992 by the Association for the Protection and Research of European

Medicinal Plants. *A. ursinum* contains more ajoene and twenty times more adenosine than cultivated garlic – substances which are known to reduce blood cholesterol and to lower blood pressure. Research by Professor Holger Kiesewetter at Homburg University Clinic, Germany, found that one gram of Wild Garlic taken daily could improve blood circulation (*Herbalpedia*). Indeed, *Herbalpedia* tells us: "In both in vitro and animal experiments, similar to *Allium sativum*, the drug has exhibited lipid-reducing and hypotensive effects, aggregation-inhibiting effects, and cardioprotective effects." In 1989, *A. ursinum* was celebrated as 'the new star' of the garlic world in German health journal *Therapy Week* (*Therapiewoche*).

Wild Garlic is not only a heart protector and blood purifier, it also cleanses and improves digestion, which is helpful to various ailments from skin disorders (such as acne, eczema and fungal infections) to stomach problems (such as diarrhoea, colic, gas, indigestion and loss of appetite). It also boosts the body's immune system and can be used as an aid to weight loss. The bruised plant releases a chemical called allicin that acts against microorganisms. Allen and Hatfield suggest this supports its use in herbalism for coughs, colds, flu and sore throats. The wild herb can has also been used as an infusion (ingested or as an enema) against threadworm.

Present-day herbals also recommend Wild Garlic as a stomach tonic, and for conditions that benefit from improved flow of bile and increased urination. Its stimulating, expectorant and antiseptic properties also make it a useful herb for catarrh or other conditions exacerbated by an overproduction of mucus in the body, and respiratory disorders such as asthma, bronchitis, and emphysema; it may also be helpful for fevers. It can be used to relieve cramps, tackle obesity, and treat abscesses and boils. Externally, the juice can be rubbed on the skin to stimulate circulation or to relieve rheumatism and arthritis.

As a healing herb, Wild Garlic can be drunk as a tea, taken as a macerated oil (for example, in olive oil), or eaten raw in salads and sandwiches. Another advantage Wild Garlic has over cultivated garlic is that it's almost odourless after consumption; although the plant itself has a strong aroma, its flavour is milder and won't give you 'garlic breath'.

It's even recommended for cats and dogs – the chopped leaves can be mixed with pet food to prevent worms – and for horses, mixed with fodder to repel flies and help to prevent 'summer eczema' to which horses are prone.

SAFETY NOTE

Duke (2002) warns that overindulgence in the herb could cause side effects such as flatulence and heartburn. Another hazard is the potential blood-thinning effects of the plant, which could make it unsuitable for people already taking blood-thinning medication or who are at risk of a condition affected by blood thinning.

The Complete German Commission E Monographs warns that people who are allergic to the Allium family may experience foul breath, rare gastrointestinal tract irritations, or other allergic reactions as a result of taking Wild Garlic. Further, the sulphides in the plant might also irritate the gastrointestinal tract or cause dermatosis.

BOTANICAL PROFILE

Scientific Name: *Allium ursinum.*

Family: Amaryllidaceae.

Botanical Description

Height: up to 50 cm. Flowers: tiny clusters of star-like, white flowers. Leaves: long, spear-shaped, fresh green leaves. Root and stem: onion-like sprouting a triangular stem.

Flowers: April to June.

Status: Perennial. Native.

Habitat: Deciduous woodland, hedgerows, riverbanks.

Ramsons (*Allium ursinum*)

11
SEA BEET

Sea Beet (*Beta vulgaris* subsp. *maritima*) is the wild ancestor to common vegetables such as beetroot, swiss chard and spinach beet. We can even thank the rugged coastal plant for the sugar in our cup of tea or coffee because it was the original to sugar beet too. The coastal plant belongs to the pigweed family, or formerly the goosefoot family, and is one of many subspecies of beet (*Beta vulgaris*) that have developed over the past two thousand years.

While the bright crimson slices of beetroot are more familiar on our plate, Sea Beet is an ancient food and medicine plant. It has been used since prehistory, but over time it has relinquished its place at the table in favour of its cultivated cousins. The origin of beet (*Beta*) species is thought to be the Middle East, from where they spread along the Atlantic sea coast to the Mediterranean.

FOOD

Sea Beet has been used as a raw vegetable or potherb since prehistory. It's speculated that its bright green leaves appearing in winter were sometimes mistaken for other plants. Biancardi, Panella and Lewellen (2012) tell us: "It is quite possible that Sea Beet (or one of its earlier relatives) already was known to our ancestors in their remote African dawn." Evidence of its use in ancient communities, including remains of seeds, stalks and roots, is widespread, and has been found at sites from the late Mesolithic era in Denmark and The Netherlands to Neolithic sites in Holland and Poland. Remains of the plant dated between 3100–2400 BC have also been collected from archeological sites in Egypt. Hunter-gather tribes may have cooked the roots after the discovery of fire, and included Sea Beet as an important part of their vegetable diet.

The cultivation of beets is thought to have begun in Mesopotamia around 8000 BC. The first cultivation occurred in Asia Minor, eventually spreading to Mediterranean areas. The practice led to the development of the wide variety of beet species known today. The wild Sea Beet (*B. maritima*) growing along coastal regions is often hailed as the originator of swiss chard, beetroot, spinach beets and so on. However, some studies suggest that the original ancestor may have been quite different to the current wild species.

In ancient Persia, gardeners admired the sturdy roots of Sea Beet that clung to sandy shores. They grew it for the large, green leaves that served well as a vegetable. As the plant diversified, newer subspecies may have replaced their ancient ancestor, but the practice of collecting the wild Sea Beet has survived from generation to generation in some parts. Why did this already remarkable vegetable require modification? It is thought that the deep, hard roots of the original Sea Beet were difficult to harvest and too woody to eat, thus the plant required selection for food. The leaves, on the other hand, were said by Pliny (c70 AD) to work well with beans, lentils and mustard. Fast forward to the 1800s and Sea Beet and its descendants had come a long way, with beet varieties already being cultivated for sugar production in Germany, for example.

A fan of the original Sea Beet, Richard Mabey (1978) commented that its large leaves are unusual for a wild vegetable as they are as "heavy as those of any cultivated spinach" and they "creak like parchment when you touch them." He encourages us to look closely at the seaside plants found today: "If you look closely at some of the wild specimens you will occasionally find a red-veined individual that is from the strain that was developed into the beetroot."

"Of all our sea-side plants, boiled for table vegetables", said Pratt in 1856, the one that most deserved commendation "is the Sea Beet". He went on to praise the plant's succulent green leaves: "This seaside spinach is certainly very wholesome, and if it were not a wild plant would be in much request." And while the roots of red beet are still more popular today, it was reported by Atheneus, a Greek rhetorician and grammarian who lived around the end of the second and beginning of the third century AD, that the roots of Sea Beet have a "sweet taste and grateful, much better than cabbage".

From the ancient world to more recent times, Sea Beet was once gathered on Irish shores and brought home to cook like spinach. The tradition survives today and the plant is known as 'sea spinach', which makes a useful winter and spring vegetable that is sold in many Irish coastal towns. Peter Wyse Jackson (2014) tells us: "I have seen it sold in organic and farmers' markets in Ireland, such as in Milltown, Co. Kerry, in April 2009." In County Cork and other coastal regions, it was cultivated in gardens as a spinach substitute. In England, some people cultivated Sea Beet in their gardens from seed gathered from wild plants.

Roy Vickery (1995) recorded anecdotes of collecting Sea Beet within other coastal communities:

On the Isles of Scilly - "Young leaves of Sea Beet are collected and boiled as spinach" Woodnewton, Northamptonshire, June 1992

St Saviour, Jersey, May 1993 - "Sea Beet is still collected when young by some people for use as spinach."

In the Isle of Wight, the leaves of Sea Beet were called 'wild spinach' or 'sea spinach' and collected by villagers to eat with pork or bacon.

Mrs Grieve (1931) wrote that the wild edible was "equal in taste to Spinach" when boiled. François Couplan (1998) went further, saying that the wild Sea Beet was superior in flavour to cultivated beets and chard, while Mabey wrote that the leaves of the wild beet changed little in cultivation "except to lose some of their powerful tannin-and-iron flavour". He recommended picking the leaves between April and October and using exactly as you would spinach. Like spinach, Sea Beet reduces in cooking and for that reason many leaves need to be gathered. The water in which it's boiled can be saved as a nutritious vegetable stock.

Sea Beet is a traditional wild vegetable in Mediterranean countries such as Spain, Portugal, Greece, Cyprus, Croatia, Bosnia-Herzegovina, Turkey, Tunisia and Jordan. The young, tender leaves can be eaten raw in salads. Older leaves are best steamed or boiled like spinach, and can be used to make a sea spinach tart or a warm vegetable salad with diced tomatoes and grated nuts. In Mediterranean cooking, the young leaves gathered in spring are cooked similarly to chard, and are considered more tender and tastier than cultivated vegetables. They are typically served with olive oil, lemon or vinegar. The plant is also prepared in bean stews, soups, omelettes, pies, and in regional dishes. Other ideas for cooking Sea Beet include broth-like soups and vegetable-and-cheese flans.

In Italy, Sea Beet is commonly gathered in the wild, and the leaves can be mixed with cheese to prepare a traditional dish similar to tortellini, or cooked with scrambled eggs. It is part of the ingredients of two popular dishes from Sardinia, Italy, and Valencia-Alicante, Spain, called *'minestra delle 18 erbe'* (eighteen greens soups) and *cocas* or *mintxos*, a pizza filled with fish and wild greens. In Cyprus, Sea Beet is one of eleven herbs used to make a traditional pie called *'pittes'*.

In Tunisia, the roots were once ground and mixed with flour to make bread in times of famine. In France, the leaves were mixed with sorrel to balance the bitter taste. In Russia, the plant was used as a base for the soup *borscht*.

Of course, tastes differ for wild edibles. The large roots of Sea Beet have a sweet flavour, wrote Jackson, but Grieve stated that they were "coarse and unfit" for food. Whatever your preference, Sea Beet has been found to contain high levels of vitamin C – about 36 mg per 100 g (de Cortes Sánchez-Mata, 2016) – although not all Sea Beet is made equal. Studies have shown that wild Sea Beet cultivated in Crete has a higher vitamin C content than that found in other regions. The fresh young leaves are also high in vitamins K (988 mg per 100 g) and B (302 μg per 100 g), and nutrients such as calcium (67 mg per 100 g), zinc (845 μg per 100 g), and iron (almost 3 mg per 100 g) (de Cortes Sánchez-Mata, 2016 again). The leaves are also rich in vitamin A. It is a good source of dietary fibre.

The culinary uses of Sea Beet's descendants like swiss chard, spinach beet and beetroot are well known. Beetroot, for example, can be pickled and eaten with almost anything, from roast dinners to burgers. It can also be steamed or boiled and eaten with butter, or grated raw for salads. Why not use Sea Beet as a substitute for these common vegetables in a multitude of recipes? Other reports say that Sea Beet has also been used as a pickle and even a coffee substitute.

Modern research into Sea Beet has observed its ability to grow in salty soils, which might prove an advantage to crop-growing when better soils are unavailable in famine-struck countries. Other research has pointed towards Sea Beet's useful resistance to certain crop diseases – a trait which has disappeared during the domestication of its descendants.

RECIPES

Sea Beet Bubble and Squeak

- 8oz sea beet tops (shredded)
- 24oz potatoes (diced)
- big dollop of butter
- salt and pepper

Boil the potatoes until soft, then mash with salt and pepper. Steam the sea beet while the potatoes are cooking, when done combine both together. Heat a frying pan and melt butter, then fry the mixture until brown on one side, then turn over and fry until also brown. Serves 2.

Sea Beet Bhijia Curry

- 500g sea beet (sliced)
- 1 onion (sliced)
- 2 red chillies (chopped)
- 350g cherry tomatoes (quartered)
- 2 garlic cloves (sliced)
- 1tbsp cumin seeds

- 1tbsp black pepper corns
- 2cms piece of fresh ginger (skinned and chopped)
- ½ tsp whole cloves
- 1tbsp turmeric powder
- 2tsp ghee or vegetable oil
- sea salt to taste

Cut the onion into thin slices, then wash the sea beet and remove the stalks from the leaf blade, chop the leaf and set aside, then chop the stalks and set aside in different pile. Next grind the cloves, cumin seeds and black pepper corns either in an electric spice or coffee grinder or by hand using a mortar and pestle.

Then heat the ghee and lightly fry the garlic along with the onion, chillies, ginger, ground cloves, cumin and black pepper, and chopped sea beet stalks. Stir continuously while frying until the sea beet stalks are starting to soften and the onion is translucent. Turn the heat down, then stir in the tomatoes, salt, and sea beet leaves. At this stage depending on how thick everything is you might want to add a dash of water, then put a lid on and let it simmer very slowly until everything is cooked. I like my sea beet well done in this recipe, but the choice is yours. Serves 2.

Wild Sea Beet Salad

- 3 large handfuls of very young sea beet (either whole or sliced)
- 2 large handfuls of oxeye daisy leaves (chopped finely)
- 2 ripe avocados (diced)
- 1 tin of green olives (whole)
- 1 lime (scrap the zest off)
- 1/2 pineapple (diced)
- vinaigrette dressing
- Olive oil

Wash the sea beet, spin dry and put in large salad bowl. Dice the pineapple, removing any of the outer skin and bristles. Add to salad bowl. Chop or shred the oxeye daisy leaves. Add to salad bowl along with the diced avocado. Add the olives, then and the lime zest, vinaigrette dressing and olive oil. Salt and pepper, then shuffle the salad to mix everything together. Allow to sit at room temperature for 20 minutes before serving to allow the flavours to infuse. Serves 3 people.

MEDICINE

It's remarkable that even John Gerard, the great English herbalist, was apparently unfamiliar with Sea Beet, although he was full of praise for its descendent, the beetroot, which was "full of perfect purple juice tending to rednesse". He grew a plant in his garden from seeds acquired from a foreign merchant named Lete. The beetroot reportedly grew to twelve feet high and the leaves were good to eat in oil, vinegar and pepper.

With this in mind, many of the references to beets in old herbals refer to subspecies such as beetroot or to the beet family in general. The Anglo-Saxon text, the *Lacnunga,* for example, has an early reference for using beets as a cure for headaches: "Roots of beet, pound with honey; wring out. Apply the juice over the nose. Let him (the patient) be face upward toward the hot sun and lay the head downward until the brain be reached. Before that, he should have butter or oil in the mouth, the mucus to run from the nose. Let him do that often until it be clean".

The wild plant is not mentioned by Dioscorides (first century AD) or Theophrastus (third century BC) who instead discuss cultivated beets, but some written records can be found which refer directly to Sea Beets. Biancardi and team (2012) wrote of: "A pupil of Aristotle, who included its dried leaves in a medicinal mixture with other herbs." The prominent Greek physician Galen even wrote that wild beet was more effective than cultivated varieties. Various references to wild beets suggest the leaves were once chewed for an eye disease (probably glaucoma), a poultice of the root was rubbed under foot to treat sciatica or was rubbed on the wrists for scabies, and the juice was said to cure the bites of wolves. In some Arabic texts it was recorded that Sea Beet juice was a remedy for ulcerations of the nostrils, hair loss, lice and dandruff. The actions of wild beet juice (although vaguely referring to *B. maritima*) were recorded in the *Herbarium of Crateuas* (around 100 BC) for relieving headaches and ear pain, removing dandruff, soothing chilblains, skin sores and itching caused by alopecia, and treating leprosy.

Several references to Sea Beet as part of a remedy for colic are mentioned in early herbals, such as Jean Ruel's *Diosciridae pharmacorum* (1529), and in a later translation of a manuscript by renowned Arabian physician Ibn Sina, or Avicenna (980–1037 AD), *Liber canonis medicinae* (1845).

A decoction was made from the seed or juice, or other parts of the plant were prepared to treat tumours, leukaemia, breast and womb cancers, and other cancers such as in the stomach, prostate, head or spleen. The leaves and root were once used as an emmenagogue – to induce menstruation.

Mrs Grieve in *A Modern Herbal* (1931) described the medicinal uses of 'white beet', 'red beetroot' and 'sugar beet'. She quotes Nicholas Culpeper (1653): "The juice of the White Beet was stated to be 'of a cleansing, digestive quality,' to open obstructions of the liver and spleen, and, wrote Culpeper, 'good for the headache and swimming therein and all affections of the brain.'" The white varieties were also recommended for poisonous stings or bites, eye inflammations, skin complaints like chilblains and blisters, dandruff and hair loss. The juice of red beetroot, on the other hand: "was recommended 'to stay the bloody flux' and 'to help the yellow jaundice.' Also the juice 'put into the nostrils, purgeth the head, helpeth the noise in the ears and the toothache.'"

Sea Beet is popular in Ayurvedic and Unani medical traditions. The leaves can be used to treat burns and bruises, and both the roots and leaves are thought to be a remedy for fatty liver, hepatitis, jaundice, nausea, diarrhoea, dysentery, constipation, haemorrhoids, anaemia, and other complaints. The seeds have been sold in Indian and Iranian bazaars for various medical uses, and a decoction of the leaves has been used in South Africa for haemorrhoids.

Modern herbals often list the actions and uses of beet subspecies collectively. The conditions broadly indicated for treatment by 'beets' are anaemia, bruising, burns, inflammation, water retention, gas, fever and various cancers. Research from Hungary suggests that beets may have anti-cancerous properties. The juice is said to catalyse oxygen and prevent tumours, while being high in iron and silicic acid that helps to regenerate red blood cells. Sea Beet, specifically *B. maritima*, is used as a medicinal plant in regions along the border of Spain and Portugal. It is recommended for digestive disorders, burns, throat pains and anaemia. In Italy, Sea Beet is eaten as a medicinal food in soups to treat constipation. In Spain, it's also eaten to relieve constipation and stomach pains or digestive complaints. Another remedy, this time from Russia, suggests gargling beet juice as a remedy for problems with the adenoids.

In veterinary herbal medicine, Sea Beet may be used to treat roundworm in cats.

SAFETY NOTE

Duke (1985) wrote that excessive use of beets could cause hypocalcemia, kidney damage or toxicity from the plant oxalates. Sánchez-

Mata and Tardío (2016) measured it at around 581 mg per 100 g) and should be avoided by people who suffer from kidney stones or renal problems.

BOTANICAL PROFILE

Scientific Name: *Beta vulgaris subsp. maritima.*

Family: Amaranthaceae.

Botanical Description

Height: up to 60 cms. Flowers: numerous spikes of bright, emerald green flowers. Leaves: large, fleshy, glossy deep-green leaves; triangular to egg-shaped. Some leaves turn purple and crimson in autumn. Root: thick fleshy root.

Flowers: June to September.

Status: Perennial. Native.

Habitat: Seashore, wasteland.

Sea Beet (*Beta vulgaris subsp. maritima*)

12

SMOOTH SOWTHISTLE

The hollow stem of sowthistle yields a white, milky juice, said to be eaten by sows to increase the flow of their milk. The Latin name of the genus 'sowthistle' is '*Sonchus*', meaning 'hollow'. There are many species of *Sonchus* – all are edible, and most are indistinguishable in appearance, but the two most commonly used for food and medicine are Smooth Sowthistle (*S. oleraceus*) and Prickly Sowthistle (*S. asper*).

Sowthistles are sometimes confused with Dandelions because of the appearance of their bright yellow flowers and green, spiny leaves. They may be mistaken for Milk Thistle due to the creamy sap, but sowthistles are unrelated to true Milk Thistle (*Silybum marianum*).

The sowthistle has a complicated relationship with humans. It has flourished in the path of human progress to become a common weed and wild edible. Along the way, some people have become devoted to its tender young leaves and juicy stem, while others have found its bitterness less agreeable.

Other common names used for sowthistle have included 'sprout thistle', because its milky shoots were a nourishing spring vegetable, and 'turn-sole', because its flowers turned to follow the sun in the sky.

One of its country names is 'hare thistle', due to the hare's fondness for the weed. The first illustrated text on herbal medicine in English, *The Grete Herball* (1526), describes Smooth Sowthistle as the 'hare's house' or 'hare's bush', because it provides a safe haven for the hare and saves the animal from its melancholy.

FOOD

Sowthistle is an ancient herb that has been picked and prepared for salads and potherbs since the days of our early ancestors. It's thought from records of seeds found at Roman settlements that the Romans introduced sowthistle to Britain as a culinary herb. In the Middle Ages, Smooth Sowthistle was sometimes collected as a green vegetable to fill the winter gap, according to English naturalist John Ray (1627–1705), rather than leaving it to be "masticated by hares and rabbits" (quoted in Grigson, 1996). Sowthistle produces several crops during its growing season if the soil is disturbed, which is an advantage as it can mean multiple opportunities to pick younger leaves and shoots rather than the less desirable older, tougher and more bitter plants.

The genus has been unfairly judged over the years as an overly bitter, tough, and spiny vegetable, perhaps due to a lack of understanding about which species to pick and when. While sowthistles can become tougher and more bitter as they mature, picked young, some species are only mildly bitter and quite succulent. Donald Watts is not a big fan; he wrote (in 2007) that sowthistle is "despised these days as a food plant, but it was not always so". He finds the sowthistle "not very interesting," but will cook it in stews and casseroles with stronger tasting herbs and vegetables.

For those who appreciate sowthistle's unruly qualities, understanding when and how to collect the plant goes a long way. For example, the stems are best picked before flowering, then peeled to be eaten raw or steamed. Of the two species most commonly collected for food – Prickly Sowthistle (*S. asper*) and Smooth Sowthistle (*S. oleraceus*) – Prickly Sowthistle is widely recognised as the bitterest herb, sometimes requiring two changes of water even when cooking the younger shoots. Smooth Sowthistle is also recognised as the more versatile vegetable. The young leaves can be mixed with salad; cooked to make soups, soufflés, and frittatas; or boiled and served like spinach. *Herbalpedia* (2014) suggests Smooth Sowthistle has the nicest tasting leaves of the lot, with a "mild agreeable flavour especially in the spring"; the stems can be cooked like asparagus or rhubarb; the young roots can be cooked, but are "woody and not very acceptable".

Whether collecting Prickly or Smooth Sowthistle, bear in mind that both the leaves and stems are perfectly edible and even the flowers can be added to salads, cooked like vegetables, added to stir fries, or dried and frozen for later use. Most herbal texts recommend 'milking' the juicy stem before preparation and cooking; the juice can turn parts of the plant brown if left inside the stem.

Fresh is best. Whichever species is collected, foragers advise using the plant as soon as possible or spray-misting before storing in a plastic bag in the fridge. This is recommended whether choosing younger or older plants; though younger plants are always preferred.

Samuel Thayer is a true devotee of sowthistle. He first became acquainted with the weed when he found it growing in the surroundings of his log cabin in northern Wisconsin. Thayer

(2006) tells us that North America is home to three common species of sowthistle: *S. arvensis*, *S. oleraceus*, and *S. asper*; all closely related to Dandelions and wild lettuce. (As an aside, the roots of sowthistles can be used as a coffee substitute like Dandelion root, although they're said to be a poorer substitute.) Traditionally, bitter herbs like Dandelion, Chicory and Marsh Marigold have been more popular in North American herbals, mentions Thayer, which he feels is due to a failure to distinguish between different species of sowthistle and find a preference. Thayer finds the taste of sowthistle "reminiscent of both Dandelion and lettuce, but there is another pleasant flavour peculiar to this genus".

Field or Perennial sowthistles find least favour with Thayer due to their bitter leaves (even when young) and thin stalks. Prickly Sowthistle produces tender stalks that are sweet and mild (in younger plants), but the spiny leaves become a "drawback". He rates Smooth or Common Sowthistle most highly for its succulent, mildly sweet stems that are excellent as snacks, added to salads, stir-fried or steamed. It is "probably the best of our three species".

François Couplan (1998) showed his appreciation of the younger plants of *S. oleraceus*, *S. asper* and *S. arvensis*, which can be collected from root to tip for salads and cooking. He advised how to manage all parts of the plant, from avoiding the older, spiny leaves of *S. asper* to preparing the roots in a food processor to eliminate the fibres. (The tap root, stripped of its fibrous parts, can be boiled and eaten like potatoes.)

John Kallas (2010) is a reformed advocate of sowthistles. He once avoided the plant for its bitter taste, but was won over by its "impressive capabilities" and looked "forward to eating it every year". He wrote that sowthistle is: "A delightful food that is one of the most widely used wild edibles in the Mediterranean". While he recognises that Prickly Sowthistle has similar properties, his preference is for Smooth Sowthistle: "Spiny [prickly] sowthistle is like the wild misbehaving brother of Smooth Sowthistle".

Kallas fully understands how to manage the plant's bitterness in cooking, which works well in "complex green, fruit and meat salads". He recommended boiling the wild greens for longer if they are to be eaten alone like spinach; the water can be drained off to use as a broth, or frozen for soup stock.

His favourite part of the plant is the thick, upper, juicy stems, which he has coined 'sowsparagus' because the flavour is like asparagus or artichoke hearts and cooked the same way. Kallas serves sowsparagus as a side vegetable dressed in a little olive oil, lemon juice and salt.

As far as wild edibles go, sowthistle appears to be enjoying a resurgence of interest. Christopher Nyerges (2014) wrote: "[sowthistles are] popularly enjoyed the world over." The herb is worthy of a variety of interesting dishes. Its chopped leaves can be cooked with onions, rice, walnuts and butter; leaves can simply be cooked like spinach; or stems cooked like asparagus. Stanley J Key's *Cultivated vegetables of the world* lists four different types of sowthistle that are eaten, including *S. asper*, *S. oleraceus*, *S. wightianus* and *S. malaianus*.

Sowthistle has been a traditional wild herb of the Mediterranean for generations. The young, tender leaves lend a bitter, nutty flavour to salads and offer another wild edible for rejuvenating spring dishes such as *pistic*. The leaves are good fodder for salads and soups in Turkey, Egypt, Spain, Italy, Sicily, Tunisia, Crete, and Cyprus. The plant is used in various traditional recipes: added to *misticanza* salad in Italy; pan fried to season omelettes in Sicily; mixed with stuffing for wild herb and vegetable pies in eastern Spain; and used as a pizza topping in Latium, western Italy. The flowers are used to curdle milk in some regions of Italy. In parts of Sicily – Caltanisetta, Vittoria and Partanna – the leaves are eaten as a medicinal food for their diuretic (increasing urination) and laxative properties. In Morocco, sowthistle is added to a springtime dish of up to twenty wild edibles called *'beqoul'*.

In South Africa, the leaves of sowthistle species (such as Smooth Sowthistle) are boiled and mixed with salt, pepper and fat to eat with bread or make into a nourishing porridge called *'imifino'*. Fox, F. M. et al. (1983) wrote in *Food from the veld* that the plant is boiled in water till soft, mixed with dough, and cooked for a couple of hours; women, children and old men eat this 'sowthistle porridge', but not, apparently, young men.

In the Nanling mountain ranges of southern China, sowthistles are gathered for food, and those who can tell the difference between the species say each has a different texture. In Nepal, prickly and smooth varieties are the sowthistles of choice – both being valued for their young, tender leaves that are cooked as vegetables. In the Himalayas, Prickly and Smooth Sowthistles are boiled in diluted milk called *'lusii'* and eaten as a vegetable.

In western parts of India, Prickly Sowthistle's spiny leaves are steamed before eating. Stephen Facciola (1998) tells us that in Indonesia an "improved type" of field sowthistle is cultivated for its leaves. He suggested that the leaves and shoots are added to curries.

In New Zealand, sowthistle was cultivated by the Maoris as a wild vegetable. The stems were milked of their bitter juice and peeled before cooking and eating; the Maoris made a chewing gum from the milky sap.

Sowthistle contains up to four times more myricetin, a polyphenolic compound, as red wine, and twelve times as many as black tea, according to Kallas (2010). It is rich in essential fatty acids and nutrients like zinc, manganese, copper, iron, calcium, and fibre. Its traditional use as an ingredient in spring dishes eaten for vitality makes sense in the light of the high levels of vitamins A, B, C, and K we now know it contains; 100 g fresh weight of various sowthistles contains between 30 and 60 mg of vitamin C (Sánchez-Mata and Tardío, 2016), and Smooth Sowthistle contains up to 800 mg of vitamin A (Kuhnlein and Turner, 1991).

While not everyone has discovered the benefits of eating sowthistle, hares and rabbits devour it with delight. Grieve (1931) wrote: "All keepers of rabbits in hutches should provide them with a plentiful supply." In County Donegal in Ireland, sowthistles have been fed to pigs and called 'swine's thistle'. Sheep and goats too are fond of sowthistle, but horses shun it. In Nepal, it is said that feeding sowthistle to pregnant animals helps the development of the fetus.

Towards the end, or beginning, of a sowthistle's life cycle – depending on your perspective – the flower heads turn into fluffy seeds that were once used to stuff pillows and mattresses in place of feathers.

Whether or not you can appreciate sowthistle at the table, fed to pets, or stuffed into cushions, Thayer's advice is to "keep your eye out for this invader [in your garden]. I'm not saying you should let it grow where you don't want it. But if you must get rid of it, do it at just the right time and get some food out of the deal".

RECIPES

Smooth Sowthistle Salsa

- 2 x garlic cloves
- 60g sow thistle
- 100g soaked hazelnuts
- 15g parsley
- ¼ teaspoon of sea salt

- 2 teaspoons of Korean red chilli flakes
- 4 tablespoons of olive oil
- 10 cherry tomatoes (chopped)

Soak the hazelnuts in boiling water for 60 minutes. Strain and rinse thoroughly. Soak the sow thistle in cold water for 60 minutes. Then remove the leaf blades from the larger leafs, discarding the leaf stalks. Don't bother doing this with the smaller leaves, as their stalks will not have become stringy.

Crush the garlic cloves and allow to sit for 15 minutes. This "triggers an enzyme reaction that boosts the healthy compounds in garlic." In a food processor add the hazelnuts, shredded sow thistle, parsley, garlic, sea salt, olive oil, red Korean chilli flakes. Then pulse until chopped and mixed up. You want a thick consistency, not runny.

Now chop the tomatoes put in a bowl and spoon out the sow thistle mixture. Fork the tomatoes through the salsa. Then serve as a sauce with your favourite dish. Traditionally served with grilled meat, but for plant-based folks, I recommend serving with nut loaf, baked tempeh, roast vegetables and/or potatoes etc. Serves 4.

Sow Thistle Capers

- Sowthistle flower buds
- 50ml white wine vinegar
- 2tsp ginger (grated)
- ½ red chilli (chopped)
- 20 ml water
- 3g sea salt
- 2.5g honey

Combine the vinegar, ginger, chilli, water, sea salt and honey and bring to a simmer then turn off and allow to infuse and cool. Put the sow thistle buds into some clean, sterile jars and top up with the cold pickling liquid. Cap and store for a month before using.

Sowthistle Tempeh Salad

- 150g young smooth sowthistle greens (chopped)
- 300g white cabbage (shredded)
- 2tbsp sesame seeds
- 2tbsp pumpkin seeds
- 2tbsp linseed seeds
- 2 garlic cloves (chopped)
- 350g tempeh (cubed)
- 1tsp vegan stock powder
- 2 red chillies (sliced)
- 2tbsp tamari
- 1 cup fresh coriander (finely chopped)
- 1/2 cup fresh mint (finely chopped)
- 1/2 cup vegetable oil
- 1/2 cup of water

Toast the seeds in a pan and then grind in a pestle and mortar and then transfer to a salad bowl. Steam the white cabbage until soft, then the sowthistle until wilted. Heat the oil in a wok, add the tempeh and fry until golden brown. Put in a pestle and mortar and smash it up, then transfer to the salad bowl. Add some more oil to the wok and fry the garlic until just beginning to go golden, then add the water and tamari, add the cooked cabbage and sowthistle greens, along with the tempeh and seeds, and chillies and fry for a couple of minutes. Then return to the salad bowl. Now add the coriander and mint and stir in well. Serves 3.

MEDICINE

John Gerard (1597) wrote about ten different kinds of sowthistle and quoted Galen in his description of their attributes: "The Sow-thistles, as Galen writeth, are of a mixed temperature; for they consist of a watery and earthie substance, cold, and likewise binding". He recommended the herb for satisfying hunger, increasing breast milk, and as generally helpful for improving health.

The medicinal virtues of Smooth Sowthistle (*S. oleraceus*) were believed to be similar to Dandelion (*Taraxacum officinale*). Its juicy stem oozed a creamy milk like Dandelion, which, also like Dandelion, was used as a cure for warts. In Ireland, sowthistles were picked to treat warts and burns. In Wales, the association between sowthistle and pigs was particularly strong, and it was thought the plant healed wounds caused by the bite or kick of a pig.

In sympathetic magic, consuming the milky sap of sowthistle had a connection to increasing the flow of milk in nursing mothers – human or sow. In the thirteenth century, Prickly Sowthistle was said to "prolong the virility of gentlemen" (Mitich, 1988). The correspondence between the plant's milky sap and male virility may fall under the Doctrine of Signatures, which assigned healing properties to plants that resembled parts of the body. James Duke (1992) tested the theory by adding the flowers of a species of sowthistle from Maryland, North America, to his diet. Unfortunately, he reported that "[I] detected no significant changes in [my] virility following ingestion of sowthistle flowers, and suspect they might be more effective against jaundice and cirrhosis than against impotency."

Traditionally, sowthistle juice was a cosmetic remedy used since ancient times. The Greeks and Romans chose it as a treatment for eye ailments and skin problems. The distilled water of the plant was used to cleanse skin and clear the complexion. Centuries later, (Culpeper and Foster, 2019) wrote that: "It is wonderful good for women to wash their faces with, to clear the skin, and give it a lustre," and that "the herb bruised or the Juice is profitably applied to all hot inflammations in the Eyes" (quoted in Watts, 2007). The juice of Prickly Sowthistle was used by South African settlers to clear complexions and as a treatment for external ulcers. Mrs Grieve in *A Modern Herbal* (1931) tells us: "the milky juice of all the Sow-Thistles is an excellent cosmetic".

As a medicinal plant, sowthistle was considered both powerful and gentle in action. It treated 'gravel and stone' in the body, referring to urinary stones, and cramps. The bitter leaves were chewed to freshen foul breath. Yet sowthistle water was believed gentle enough for those with very sensitive stomachs.

Historically, the different species of sowthistle don't appear to have much difference between them in folk medicine. Grieve tells us that Field, or Perennial Sowthistle (*S. arvensis*) can bring down swellings, and Mountain Sowthistle (*S. alpinus*) was valued for its milky juice. David Allen and Gabrielle Hatfield (2007) noted that the only record of use that can be attributed to a specific species was *S. arvensis* in Lincolnshire, England. They wrote:

> "Probably all three [*S. oleraceus, S. asper* and *S. arvensis*] share much the same properties, in particular the white juice that has given rise to the names 'milkweed', 'milkwort' and 'milk thistle' in England and Ireland alike and been widely applied to warts in both countries."

A historian of plant medicine, Hatfield (2007) tells us sowthistle is not much used in present-day herbalism. The plant is most cited as an age-old remedy for warts by cutting the milky stem and rubbing the juice on the wart.

In Western herbal medicine today, sowthistle is a useful herb for women's health. It is classed in the group of plants known as emmenagogues, because it is thought to bring on menstruation and therefore can be helpful in regulating infrequent periods. The roots of Perennial Sowthistle (*S. arvensis*) are specifically mentioned in a remedy to increase the flow of breastmilk in nursing mothers; an extract is taken from the roots crushed in watered rice. An infusion of the plant is said to treat diarrhoea.

In North American herbalism, Smooth Sowthistle juice is considered useful for digestive problems.

The herb is valued in the natural health and beauty industry for cleansing the skin, inside and out. *Herbalpedia* states: "Countrywomen add an eggcupful of juice to a pint of warmed rain water and apply it to the face at night." In addition, sowthistle is thought to help detoxify the liver which helps to purify the skin. The herb has also been used in eye drops.

In traditional Chinese medicine, sowthistle has similar uses. It was regarded as a nourishing vegetable that could bestow health and vitality. The juice is used to treat warts, boils and abscesses. An infusion of the flowers, leaves and roots treat a fever.

In the Himalayas, Smooth Sowthistle leaves are made into a decoction and taken to relieve constipation and to strengthen the body. The plant is also recommended for diarrhoea, menstrual disorders, fever and inflammation of the body. Prickly Sowthistle leaves are decocted for constipation and fever, and a leaf paste can be applied topically for boils and wounds.

Further uses for sowthistle are found in other species of the genus. Perennial Sowthistle (*S. arvensis*) is used to treat an acid stomach by chewing or making a paste from the roots; the crushed leaves treat cuts and boils; the crushed seeds treat coughs and fevers; and the juice is indicated for nervousness and heart palpitations. Perennial Sowthistle may be a helpful anti-inflammatory for boils, haemorrhoids and skin eruptions. *S. brachyotus* juice can be taken for fevers and convulsions, and the whole plant is said to relieve pain. Finally, *S. dregeanus* may be given to breastfeeding mothers and recommended for skin rashes in babies.

One of the most extraordinary claims for sowthistle (referring once again to the most commonly used species) is reported in *Herbalpedia*: "Around the turn of the century the Chinese in the San Francisco area used an evaporated extract of the white milky sap of sowthistle as an antinarcotic to help break opium addiction." The latex in the sap is also said to have anticancer activity.

In veterinary medicine, sowthistle might be used to treat diarrhoea and vaginal prolapse.

SAFETY NOTE

All powerful-acting herbal medicines should be treated with respect. *Herbalpedia* suggests that the juice of sowthistle is so potent it might cause colic or tenesmus (a disorder of the rectum and bowels). The plant might also contain toxic levels of nitrates and should be used with caution.

Smooth Sowthistle is considered slightly more toxic than other species of sowthistle, according to Umberto Quattrocchi's *World Dictionary of Medicinal and Poisonous Plants* (2012). A white latex produced from the plant is mildly poisonous to lambs and horses, and the roots are said to induce abortion.

BOTANICAL PROFILE

Scientific Name: *Sonchus oleraceus.*

Family: Compositae.

Botanical Description

Height: up to 150 cm. Flowers: pale yellow flowers similar to dandelion heads; wither to form a conical with tufty seeds. Stem: thick-branched, hollow stem; yields a white milky juice. Leaves: thin, oblong leaves with prickly-teeth edges. Fruit: appear like a small ribbed nutlet.

Flowers: April to December.

Status: Annual. Native.

Habitat: Cultivated land, wasteland.

Smooth Sowthistle (*Sonchus oleraceus*)

13
SORREL

The common sorrel is a plant of many names. One of its most charming is cuckoo's meat, because of an old belief that it cleared the cuckoo's throat and restored the bird's iconic bubbling cackle. There is such a variety of sorrels, and such a cornucopia of local names, that you may be forgiven for some confusion over which species is which in different herbals. In this chapter, common sorrel (*Rumex acetosa*) is the star of the show, although some of its closely related cousins make a guest appearance.

Its most familiar namesake 'sorrel' is from the French '*surele*', rooted in '*sur*' and meaning 'sour'. Other local names, such as 'sooricks', 'sour grabs' and 'sour leeks' stem from the herb's sour taste, whether eaten raw, used in cooking or prepared as a condiment. Common sorrel was in popular use in England at the time of King Henry VIII around the sixteenth century.

As with many ordinary herbs, Culpeper felt that the English sorrel growing around and about needed no description. He declared that it was under the dominion of Venus, the planet and goddess of love in Roman mythology, with little explanation.

As a medicinal and garden herb, common sorrel has been used since the ancient days of Greece's Dioscorides and Rome's Pliny the Elder in the first century AD. Its tendency to appear as one of the first plants in spring meant it was once a highly valued edible green. Its arrow-shaped leaves were a familiar sight in medieval vegetable gardens across Europe until the 1700s, and it has since become a common wild herb in North America where it was introduced as a salad green.

FOOD

Common sorrel is almost tasteless in early spring, according to Grieve (1931), but much tastier in full season, and well known for the "grateful acidity of its herbage". She credited the plant's sour quality, as well as its medicinal and diuretic effects, to its large constituent of binoxalate potash, or oxalic acid. Sorrel's sourness was used in cooking similarly to lemons, and its sharp flavour made it a tasty addition to salads, although it might not be appreciated by everyone. Its leaves could be cooked like spinach, either lightly boiled or steamed, and their acidic flavour made an excellent side dish to red meat and roasts, or could be added to stews.

According to John Evelyn, no salad was complete without the 'quick bite' of sorrel. He wrote in 1699:

> "Sorrel sharpens the appetite … in the making of sallets imparts a grateful quickness to the rest as supplying the want of oranges and lemons. Together with salt, it gives both the name and the relish to sallets from the sapidity, which renders not plants and herbs only, but men themselves pleasant and agreeable."

It sounds like an essential addition to a summer barbecue to keep guests refreshed and in good spirits.

In old recipe books, sorrel was used to spice up bland-tasting egg dishes. In *Royal Cookery* (1710), Master Cook to Charles II, James II, William and Mary, and Queen Anne, a sorrel sauce is given for poached eggs. It was also an ingredient in egg tarts and omelettes.

Children in Dorset, England, delighted in the "refreshingly sour-tasting leaves and stems" of common sorrel, wrote Roy Vickery (1995):

> "Sour sabs–like dock with red stems–we pulled and sucked the stems"
>
> — PLYMSTOCK, DEVON, JANUARY 1993

> "As children in wartime we used to search spring meadows for the first leaves of sorrel–called sour-docks in Berwickshire–to cure our spots. We sucked the sour juice and spat out the chewed leaves."
>
> — OLD CLEEVE, SOMERSET, OCTOBER 1993

Hatfield (2007) recalls her own children would enjoy chewing sorrel leaves, which they called 'vinegar leaves', on a hot, summer's walk.

Vickery noted that sorrel was less favoured by adults in recent times. Its use as a wild herb in Britain had declined. Nevertheless, it was still used in some local recipes. Sorrel was an ingredient of 'bistort pudding', a savoury dish made with the leaves of the bistort plant at Easter, in north-west England. In Cornwall, under its West Country name of 'sour sab', it was the main ingredient in sour-sab pie, which was made with tender leaves and stalks, and served with sugar and cream.

In Ireland, of the two species of sorrel used as a culinary herb, Niall Mac Coitir (2015) wrote that common sorrel (*R. acetosa*) was picked and eaten raw, or else cooked to make soup or broth; and Peter Wyse Jackson (2014) wrote that a thirst-quenching drink could be made from sheep sorrel (*R. acetosella*) by steeping the leaves in hot water, adding a sweetener and leaving to cool.

A common name for sorrel was 'poor man's herb', which may refer to its ready availability as a herb used by country people. In the English countryside, the plant was mashed and mixed with vinegar and sugar to be served as a green sauce with cold meat, which led to another popular name: 'green sauce'. Green sauce was a favourite condiment served with fish, and a good substitute for apple sauce if served with pork or goose. Early nineteenth-century herbalist Mrs Bardswell tells us that sorrel green-sauce was used when "no apples are forthcoming" (quoted in Rohde, 1921). In Lancashire, chopped sorrel was added to suet and flour to make green sauce dumplings.

It seems that common sorrel lost its place at the table after the introduction of French sorrel, which was preferred for its larger, more succulent leaves. Both the French and English types of sorrel made excellent potherbs, but the French variety was said to be less bitter; although Grieve (1931) described its taste as more acidic.

French sorrel, or buckler-shaped sorrel (*Rumex scutatus*), is a native of the mountainous districts of southern France, Italy, Switzerland, Germany and North Africa. It was introduced to Britain in 1596. Writing under the heading of common, or garden, sorrel, Grieve tells us that the English variety of sorrel (*R. acetosa*) was used in France, despite the success of its French counterpart, as an ingredient in ragouts, fricassées and soups; it was also the main ingredient in the popular *soup aux herbes*. One can see how easy it is to become confused by different species names and their specific uses: Donald Watts (2007), for example, identified 'garden sorrel' as (*R. scutatus*). As a potherb in France, sorrel lent a strong flavour to heavy dishes of potato, lentils and haricot beans.

The variety of sorrel called 'Nobel' is most favoured amongst French chefs. In fact, sorrel was such as popular herb in France that forty-four million pounds in weight of the herb were delivered to French markets in 1895. Parisian Georges Gibault wrote in his *Histoire des Legumes* (1912) that few countries liked sorrel as much as France.

Stephen Facciola in his *Cornucopia* (1998) wrote that a purée of common sorrel (*R. acetosa*) was used in French cooking to stuff shad, a type of fish, because its oxalic acid dissolved the numerous fish bones.

The herb was popular in Belgian cooking, according to an article in *Truth* magazine in November 1916. An extract cited by Eleanour Sinclair Rohde in *A Garden of Herbs* (1921), which doesn't specify the exact species, reports: "the presence of the Belgians in England created a demand for it". It was used, similarly to spinach, to make a "famous sorrel soup", and preserved for winter use as a "delicious vegetable garnish". Sorrel is best frozen for storage because it doesn't dry well.

Sorrel is making a comeback as a versatile garden herb, according to Hatfield (2008), who herself sounds rather fond of the plant. She wrote that it gives a "delicious piquancy to soups and salads or a green sauce may be prepared from the herb, to accompany meat and poultry", and the leaves can be wrapped around tough meat to tenderise it while cooking. Facciola wrote that sorrel leaves are a pleasant addition to pease pudding (a savoury dish typically made using split yellow peas); the flowers can be cooked as a vegetable or used as garnish; and the seeds can be ground to make bread.

Nutritionally, sorrel's oxalic acid and tannins are still thought to account for its sourness, as Grieve claimed. In Italy, common sorrel was an ingredient in a wild herb mixture called *'pistic'*, usually prepared in spring. These spring tonics were once popular cures to revitalise the body after a long, cold and dark winter. Its potential as a table herb or vegetable is almost endless. Stanley Kays (2011) listed sorrel as a cultivated vegetable in several countries, including: Germany, Denmark, Norway, Finland, Iceland, Albania, Bulgaria, Hungary, Poland, Slovenia, Croatia, Greece, Africa, India, Vietnam and Arabia. The wild herb was picked in Scandinavia during times of scarcity and eaten with bread. In Lapland, it's eaten mixed with reindeer milk and the juice of the leaves is used as a rennet to curdle milk.

The species of sorrel introduced to North America from Europe (*R. acetosa* and *R. acetosella*) were recognised for their characteristic sour taste. They were consumed raw in salads or made into soups and purées.

North America's own native species of sorrel, such as *R. hymenosepalus*, *R. mexicanus*, *R. occidentalis*, *R. venosus* and *R. violascens*, were used as a food source by Native American Indians. The stems and stalks could be made into pies and compotes. The Papago Indians roasted rather than boiled sorrel leaves because of a scarcity of water.

Couplan (1998) wrote that the leaves of all sorrel species are edible, but the younger leaves are best picked for salads because they become bitter with age; after which the leaves should be boiled in a couple of changes of water to lose their astringency. He also suggested that the leaves can be cooked in milk to counteract the astringent tannins. In general use, without laying claim to any particular species, Couplan wrote that sorrel leaves can be "mixed with flour for making bread or pancakes, added to eggs for omelettes, cooked with honey as pie filling or macerated in water with some honey for a refreshing drink."

Couplan's casual references to 'sorrel' can perhaps be forgiven. Other sources agree that common sorrel (*R. acetosa*) and its closely related species, such as those distributed throughout the Mediterranean, all have a similar taste and use; although *R. acetosa* is usually cited in ethnobotanical studies.

R. acetosa root was reportedly dried and powdered in Japan to make into noodles. In China, the young leaves of *R. acetosa* are used as a potherb. In East India, sorrel is used in soups and omelettes.

Couplan listed an Arctic variety of sorrel – *R. articus* – which was eaten by the Inuits of Alaska as a type of sauerkraut.

In the Caribbean, the flowers are used to make a holiday beverage and dried to exchange at Christmas time.

RECIPES

Sorrel, Watercress and Roasted Fennel Soup

- 130 g sorrel
- 100 g watercress
- 2 medium-sized fennel
- 3 dessert spoons tamari
- 1 onion
- 1″ piece of fresh ginger (chopped)
- 2″ piece of fresh turmeric (chopped)
- 1-litre vegan stock
- 2 tablespoons of olive oil
- cracked black pepper to taste

Place the fennel in a conventional oven at 200 °C, fan-assisted 180°C or gas mark 6, and roast for 20 minutes. While the fennel is cooking, sauté the onion in a small amount of olive oil, along with the ginger and turmeric. Wash the sorrel and watercress and chop. Remove the fennel from the oven, take off any tough outer skin, and chop. In a blender add all the ingredients, and pulse, blitz, blend the mixture to your desired consistency. Some people like fine soups, others chunky. Heat and serve. Serves 2 people.

Sorrel Tartlets

For the pastry

- 250g plain flour (I like to use ½ white ½ wholemeal)
- ½ teaspoon baking powder
- 125g butter
- 1 egg
- 1 tablespoon cold water

For the filling

- 500g baby new potatoes
- 4 ttbsp olive oil
- Salt and pepper
- 2 onions, peeled and finely sliced
- 100g sorrel
- 70g mature cheddar, grated
- 200g double cream
- 2 eggs
- 6 x 12cm loose-based tartlet tins

Preheat the oven to 400°F/200°C/180 Fan. Par boil the potatoes for 10 minutes, drain, halve or quarter, then put in a roasting tin with

2 tablespoons oil, season with salt and pepper. Roast for 30 minutes and leave to cool.

Make the pastry by either putting the flour, baking powder and butter in a food processor and blitzing until the mixture resembles breadcrumbs, or do it by hand. Add the egg and water and pulse until the mixture just begins to clump, then remove and bring together with your hands. Divide the pastry into 6 even-sized pieces and roll out each one to fit the tins. Line the tins with the pastry and place in the fridge to chill until required.

Gently fry the onions with the remaining 2 tablespoons oil, stirring occasionally until they are really soft and gently coloured. Leave to cool. Whisk the eggs and cream together and season with freshly ground black pepper.

Reduce the oven to 350°F/180°C/160 Fan.

To assemble the tartlets: divide the onions between the tins then pour over half the egg mixture. Add the potatoes, prepared greens and cheese, then pour in the remaining egg/cream. Bake in the oven for 25-30 minutes or until the filling is set and golden. Serve warm. Serves 6.

Sorrel à la Bourgeoise

Pick and wash 500g of sorrel. Put in a pan with enough water to cover it and bring to a boil. Simmer for 10 minutes then strain and press as much water out of it as possible. In a saucepan, fry one chopped onion until translucent along with the sorrel, then add 1 tbsp of plain flour, ¼tsp of nutmeg or mace, 1tbsp sugar and mix together. Next add 125ml of hot stock, salt and pepper and cook for 3 minutes. Strain through a fine sieve and serve with bread.

MEDICINE

Sorrel was a treatment for 'hot' diseases because it was believed to be a 'cooling' herb. Culpeper said that it cooled inflammation and sickness arising from heat of the blood; it quenched thirst and provoked appetite; and it killed worms and cured the sting of a scorpion. He prescribed a method of use for each of various different parts of the plant: decoctions of the roots, seeds and flowers; a syrup of the juice; and a poultice of the leaves. And at the end of his sorrel entry, he added: "The distilled water of the herb is of much good use for all the purposes aforesaid".

Grieve wrote that sorrel's cooling and diuretic nature was helpful for fevers, tumorous skin diseases, jaundice, ulcerated bowels and kidney stone; on the last point, some would disagree, but we will come to that later. The root and seed were said to have an astringent action good for haemorrhages, and the juice was thought to cure itching, ringworm and a sore throat. The sting of nettles could be eased by the juice of *R. acetosa*.

John Gerard (1597) identified eight different varieties of sorrel including "garden, bunched or knobbed, sheep, Romane, curled, barren and great broad-leaved sorrel". He gave to each one the properties of 'cool', 'dry' or 'sour', which likely stem from the Doctrine of Signatures. The Doctrine ascribed qualities such as 'hot', 'cold', 'dry' and 'moist' to plants as an indication of which 'humour' they could treat in the body. Gerard wrote:

> "Sorrell doth undoubtedly cool and mightily dry, but because it is sour, it likewise cutteth tough humours. The juice thereof in summer time is a profitable sauce in many meats and pleasant to the taste. It cooleth a hot stomach. The leaves are with good success added to decoctions, and are used in agues [shivering fever]. The leaves are taken in good quantity, stamped and stained into some

ale and cooleth the body. The leaves are eaten in tart spinach. The seed of Sorrell drunk in wine stoppeth the bloody flow."

William Salmon said that sorrel's ability to cool the body and stimulate appetite was useful in treating the Plague.

Aside from its employment as a cooling and drying herb, other uses for common sorrel have emerged in folk remedies around the British Isles. Similarly to nettle and burdock, it was a blood purifier and could clear up spots. The leaves were chewed for the symptoms of epilepsy. It was sometimes mixed with other herbs, such as thistle tops and plantain, to treat consumption (tuberculosis); or with Dandelions to treat heart problems.

It was by no means a cure-all, but it was mentioned in a number of folk remedies. In Ireland, it was used to treat wounds and sickness, to heal sores and bruises, treat boils, septic sores and chickenpox, and to detox the body; it was even used to treat cancer. In Scotland, the plant was used to treat tuberculosis.

A similar species of sorrel known as sheep's sorrel (*R. acetosella*) is common in Ireland and frequents hilly and mountainous areas. It prefers the peaty soils of grasslands, heaths and cultivated grounds. Archaeological excavations in Dublin that uncovered the remains of *R. acetosella* suggest it was used in human culture more than a thousand years ago.

Sheep's sorrel was used similarly in Irish folk medicine and might be confused with common sorrel in different herbals. As a 'cooling' herb, it treated fevers and repressed bile. It was said to be diuretic, which one might expect of most common weeds described in the early herbals. It was also a remedy for scurvy, once again a familiar claim for any wild plant with a high content of vitamin C. On this last point, David Allen and Gabrielle Hatfield (2004) suggest the use of sorrel (referring specifically to common sorrel or *R. acetosa*) as a cure for scurvy – documented in the Isle of Man, Orkney, Shetlands and Faeroe Islands – seems to be Viking in origin.

Across the water in North America, native species of sorrel were harvested for their roots. Dock roots, wrote François Couplan, contain tannin, and minerals such as iron (which helps to increase red blood cell count). He explained that the roots of various sorrel species are astringent and generally good for treating wounds and ulcers.

Animals too were treated with sorrel. Hatfield (2007) quotes a source, Mrs P M–, from Selkirk, Scotland, in 2002: "I have an excitable King Charles spaniel who has a heart condition and she gets chopped sorrel leaves in her meals to calm her". A doctor from Norwich, England, in the eighteenth-century, made the (perhaps wild) connection between wild rabbits' huge consumption of sorrel and their ability to breed rapidly. He planted a sorrel patch in his garden and was said to have fathered twelve children; the twelfth child apparently being born when he was in his seventies.

German abbess Hildegard of Bingen in the twelfth century felt sorrel was more harmful than helpful to people, but said it was useful for animals because "what is harmful in it for the strength of a person is useful for the strength of animals".

Present-day herbalists may recommend sorrel as a diuretic and mild laxative, and the plant still has a reputation for healing minor wounds and bruises.

Its traditional folk uses are echoed in today's herbal medicine where it's used for skin problems and to detox the body. It's regarded as an anti-aging herb because of its calcium content. When bruised and mixed with lard, sorrel makes a poultice for corns – a remedy recorded in Illinois, North America. In *Bartram's*

Encyclopedia of Herbal Medicine (2002), its primary use is given as a treatment for bad breath.

Without distinguishing a particular species, Couplan wrote that sorrel is diuretic, laxative, good for the stomach and depurative (purifying and detoxifying) – all in moderation. James Duke wrote in his *Handbook of Medicinal Herbs* (2002): "Frankly, I think most species [of sorrel] seem to share the same chemistries and indications". He supported some uses of sorrel (*R. acetosa*) in folk medicine, noting that it is antiscorbutic (good for treating scurvy); antipyretic (cools fevers); a vermifuge and ascaricide (rids the body of worms); litholytic (dissolves stones in the body); a secretagogue (stimulates secretions); diaphoretic (promotes sweating and therefore purifies); and, of course, diuretic. He also suggested its use in herbalism for treating abscesses, wounds, inflammation and infection, constipation, diarrhoea, gallstones, earache, anaemia, diabetes, and cancer.

In Nepal, a paste of sorrel root is applied to set dislocated bones.

In veterinary medicine, common sorrel has been used as a digestive remedy and for treating worms.

SAFETY NOTE

The acidic properties of sorrel may disagree with those suffering from gout. Grieve recommended boiling in a couple of changes of water to reduce its acidic component. Likewise, over-indulgence in the plant's sour taste could upset stomachs.

Couplan wrote that the European species of *R. acetosa* and *R. acetosella* should be eaten in moderation because of their oxalic acid content, which can produce kidney stones. He recommended that people with arthritis, rheumatism, gout, inflammatory digestive problems, asthma and tuberculosis should also avoid eating sorrel.

A study by McGuffin and team (1997) concluded that sorrel (*R. acetosa*) should be used with caution in persons with a history of kidney stones. Karalliedde and Gawarammana (2008) said that consuming large amounts of sorrel leaf salad could result in oxalate poisoning.

These studies conflict with aforementioned advice in folk medicine that sorrel could be used to treat, rather than aggravate, kidney stones.

Poisoning is noted in livestock that ingest large quantities of sorrel (*R. acetosa*) due to its oxalate crystals. Sorrel that is prepared as fodder for pigs was mixed with other ingredients, such as flour and bran, to counteract is acidity.

The plant's pollen can trigger hayfever and bronchial asthma in sensitive people.

BOTANICAL PROFILE

Scientific Name: *Rumex acetosa.*

Family: Polygonaceae.

Botanical Description

Height: 10–120 cm. Flowers: several stalks bearing clusters of small reddish-green to brown flowers. Leaves: long, oblong, spear-shaped leaves and bright green. Root: fibrous.

Flowers: May to July.

Status: Perennial. Native.

Habitat: Deciduous woodland, cultivated land, grassland, hedgerows, meadow, roadsides, scrub, wasteland.

Sorrel (*Rumex acetosa*)

14
STINGING NETTLE

Nettle is easily identifiable by touch, thanks to its stinging hairs, which made it at once shunned for the burning pain it inflicted and sought after for its usefulness in folk traditions. The name 'nettle' is rumoured to come from the Anglo-Saxon word for 'needle', which refers either to its stinging hairs (needles) or its importance as a source of thread. In Holland, the name *'netel'* is perhaps derived from *'noedle'* meaning 'needle', which reflected its value for cloth-makers. Other authorities suggest its name comes from *'net'*, or from the Latin *'nassa'* meaning 'fishnet', while *'Urtica'* is from the Latin 'to sting'.

FOOD

An interesting proposition was put forward by James Duke in the *Handbook of Edible Weeds* (2000):

> "If, instead of spraying our weeds, we ate the safe ones, we would save all that energy tied up in the manufacture and application of pesticides (US farmers spend an estimated $3 billion a year

applying herbicides) and in the raising, processing, and shipping of more conventional foods."

Duke claimed, as one of the few foragers who still eats stinging nettles raw, that the nettles "quit stinging by the time they get to the throat, at least in my trials".

Indeed, nettle is a plant of extraordinary nutritional value, packed full of vitamins A, C and some Bs. In studies, 100 g of fresh nettles have been shown to contain: "670 mg potassium, 590 mg calcium, 18 mcg chromium, 270 mcg copper, 86 mg magnesium, and 4.4 mg iron" (Kress, 2011). Given that they are cheap to cultivate and grow in abundance, it's a wonder nettle products aren't flying off the supermarket shelves.

Today's herbalists and naturopaths usually recommend collecting young, tender nettles early in the year. Some herbals explain this by suggesting older nettle plants have an undesirable diuretic effect or might even be considered toxic.

A good tip when soaking wild plants before use is to add a pinch of salt to the water, which encourages small creatures to depart quicker.

Like many of our wild edible plants, nettle can be used in a wide variety of dishes. It can be substituted for spinach in salty recipes for casseroles, stews, broths, soup, and pastries. Powdered, dried nettles can be sprinkled on meals like a 'superfood' – try adding it to omelettes, baked goods and mashed potatoes.

As a spring vegetable, nettle has long been associated with health and vitality. This was recognised by the early herbalists. Buhner (1998) wrote:

> "Before the kind of food preservation we now enjoy, winter meals were usually limited to meat and stored grains, and dried plants and fruits. Scurvy was thus a recurring problem in many northern cultures. The early dark green nettle plants have always been thought of as a spring tonic and antiscorbutic remedy and were an important part of traditional diets."

A nettle pudding was made in East Anglia as a "pick-me-up after the winter" (Hatfield, 2007). In 1661 Samuel Pepys wrote in his diary.

"And there we did eat some nettle porrige, which was made on purpose to-day for some of their coming, and was very good".

Nettle porridge or pudding was a hearty dish cooked in Scotland and Ireland. It was made from nettle and oatmeal and known as *'brachan neantog'* in Ireland and 'nettle kail' in Scotland. Nettles were gathered for early spring kail until around the 1800s. In both Scotland and Ireland a nettle haggis was made.

Further afield, in the remote hilly regions of Nepal, nettle was also an important source of food. As in Europe, the shoots and leaves were gathered as a vegetable or to be made into soup. Interestingly, a type of porridge was a popular dish there too, in this case made by adding nettle to various grains with salt and chili. In the Basque country, nettle is used to strain milk for a traditional dessert, *'mamia'*, made using milk curd and rennet served with honey.

As a spring tonic, nettle has proved that food really can be medicine. It was thought to be helpful for poor circulation and anaemia, and we now know that nettle contains iron and vitamin C. Other spring tonics made with nettle, in addition to porridge and pudding, were tea and beer. Even today, nettle tea is considered delicious as well as filling and nutritious, and it can be sweetened with honey or even salted as a broth.

It's easy to understand the attraction of nettle as a spring vegetable in past times. It was readily available for harvesting after a harsh winter, and when cut back it would re-grow vigorously for a second or third spring crop. In Ulster, Ireland, its name *'cul faiche'* meant 'field cabbage'. Nettle, along with Charlock and Carrageen, was said to be one of the three plants that fed people in Ireland during the great famine. It was boiled as greens or made into soup, and the iron-rich nettle water – a by-product of cooking – was drunk.

The nettle bed was once a common feature of English gardens. Nettles were often included in recipes in Victorian cookbooks and sold in eighteenth-century markets. In 1940s Britain, nettle was a common vegetable due to rations and food shortages during the Second World War.

In short, nettle's use as a food stuff was nothing short of legendary, or so says an Irish tale about a saint who lived on nothing but the herb. The story goes that St Colmcille asked an old woman why she was cutting nettles and she replied that she lived on nettle pottage. Humbled by the old woman, the saint said he would live only on nettle pottage. But this worried his servant who secretly poured meat juice into his master's meal using a hollow pipe. Gradually St Colmcille became suspicious, but the servant maintained he used "nothing but nettles, unless something comes from the iron of the pot, or from the stick used to stir it," thus satisfying his master and keeping his conscience clear.

A similar story in Ireland tells of a St Coemgen who lived for seven years eating nothing but nettle and sorrel. In another legend, this time about the life of St Brigid, the saint fed a large number of people from an empty larder by turning nettles into butter, and tree bark into delicious food.

The customs that surround eating nettle could fill a cookbook. In Jewish traditions, nettle is one of five 'bitter herbs' of the Mishna that must be eaten at the Feast of the Passover.

In Britain, Ireland and in some European countries like Germany, Belgium, France and Italy, young nettle leaves were commonly cooked as a vegetable or used to make soup. Nettle is one of the ingredients in Maundy Thursday soup, because it was believed that gathering and eating nettle on Maundy Thursday would free you from the worldly cares of riches. In Russia, a nettle dye was used to stain eggs yellow on Maundy Thursday.

Similar customs in southern Germany, Austria and Italy meant one of the seven or nine cakes eaten on St John's Day should be nettle cake, while anyone wishing to have a good year ahead should eat nettle cake on New Year's Day. In fact, Pliny recommended that nettle was eaten to ensure good health all year round, and in Ireland it was believed that taking three meals with nettle in May would prevent illness for the rest of the year.

In a collection of Roman cookery recipes, nettle is included as a vegetable that is also recommended as a medicinal herb: "The female nettle, when the sun is in the position of Aries, is supposed to render valuable services against ailments of various kinds" (de Cortes Sánchez-Mata and Tardío, 2016).

Many superstitions surround nettles that were picked in May, which was an auspicious time of year for making lucky charms. In west Galway, a man would gather nettles on May Eve and make pressed nettle juice for his household so that they would "keep a good fire" in them in the year ahead (Mac Coitir, 2015). However, legends warned against gathering nettles after May Day, because the devil was out and about picking nettles to make his shirt.

Some European fairytales said that nettles, and thistles, were the vegetables of the devil. Whether this made nettle more or less enticing to eat is unclear, although its reputation as a 'devilish' foodstuff is quite understandable considering that raw stinging nettles were sometimes offered. In Sicily, people ate raw nettles after breaking the stinging hairs against their trouser leg.

There's little doubt that nettle is more palatable as a cooked vegetable. Thayer (2006) wrote: "Cooking nettles, even briefly, destroys their stinging property and renders them completely safe for consumption." Steamed nettle greens can reputedly be used in any recipe – from a hearty broth to a simple side dish with a little salt as an accompaniment to fish. Drying nettles is also said to destroy the stinging hairs and allows them to be sprinkled on savoury dishes for extra flavour. For those who prefer healthier snacks, nettle leaves can be blanched and eaten like sea kale.

Nettle is listed by the Council of Europe as a natural food flavouring and is approved for use in herbal teas and soups. However, in the US nettle is listed as a 'Herb of Undefined Safety' by the FDA.

Two of the most famous uses for nettle in food production are for cheese and beer, which most will agree make the perfect pair. Let's start with nettle cheese.

Nettle has a long association with dairy farmers in plant lore. Superstition led farmers to protect their herds from witches and other evil influences with nettle. In 1641, at a witch trial in Transylvania, Romania, the milk of a bewitched cow was poured onto nettle and the nettle beaten to make the witch appear. At Christmas, a nettle root was placed in milk intended for cheese-making; then, at Epiphany, the milk was poured onto a dunghill to prevent witches from cursing the dairy. In the seventeenth and eighteenth centuries, nettles were used to strike the butter churn if the butter didn't form properly. The buttermilk was then poured into a hole in the earth with a stake driven through and the nettle buried next to it. In the early to mid twentieth century, farmers in Russia, Finland and Hungary hung nettle on stable doors on St John's Day to ward off evil. In Germany, nettles gathered before sunrise would protect cattle from evil spirits. In Austria and Italy people collected nettle before dawn to protect the cattle from demonic spirits, and in Hungary people cut nettle stems on Whitsuntide eve to protect cattle from bewitchment. There was also a general belief that nettle in the house protected milk from witches and trolls.

Nettle's important role in myth and legend as a protector of milk, butter and cheese was related to its culinary use. For one thing, its juice, or a decoction of the plant, could curdle milk, making it a good source of rennet for cheese makers. Perhaps this was something that had been observed during the strange rituals that used nettle to drive away evil from the dairy.

Whatever the reasoning behind the tradition, nettle has become a useful plant in food preservation, and not only for keeping cheese. In England, nettle leaves are used to wrap mold-ripened cheese called 'Cornish Yarg'. In areas of Central Europe it's used to wrap butter and meat to keep them longer in summer. Stone fruits and tomatoes are also kept fresher for longer by pickling with nettle leaves.

In modern cheese-making, nettle has proved a palatable product for today's consumer. A study by Fiol and team (2016) found that not only was stinging nettle an acceptable alternative to vegetable coagulant rennet in cheese making, but it also opened new gastronomical possibilities for recipes in vegetarian cheeses and yoghurts. More importantly, consumer acceptance of nettle as a rennet for milk curds and cheeses would help "increase the value of a product using edible wild herbs" (Fiol and team, 2016). The researchers tested various recipes, including nettle cheese croquette, cheese wrapped in blanched nettle leaves, and sautéed vegetables mixed with nettle cream cheese.

But before you take a bite of delicious nettle cheese, consider the plant's tricky nature. While many stories tell of nettle driving off evil from dairy farms, others speak of cattle which graze on nettle yielding a bloody milk and becoming bewitched. Luckily a counter-charm is available, but it involves a long ritual using – yes, you've guessed it – nettle.

Once you've eaten a platter of nettle cheese, and hopefully escaped enchantment, you'll need a tankard of nettle beer to wash it down.

Almost as many superstitions surrounded nettle beer or ale as surrounded the dairy, and these were often associated with the plant's connection to the thunder god Thor. In Germany, nettle was placed on beer barrels to protect the brewery from being struck by lightning. There may be another explanation for this practice. Today it's known that certain chemical components in nettle affect the bacteria that break down sugars and turn them into alcohol, and that these bacteria rapidly multiply before a storm. It's possible that at some point the link was made between placing nettle in beer around the time of a summer storm and the outcome of an improved brew.

There are numerous historical records and recipes for beers and ales made with nettle, which was once a 'standard tonic' to be drunk in spring or summer.

As a tonic, nettle beer or ale was, of course, not only drunk for pleasure but for medicinal purposes. The ale was supposedly good for treating jaundice; and the beer, as made by cottagers, was drunk as an old folk remedy for gout and rheumatism. Today there are many variations of homemade nettle brew, but in general the young nettles tops are gathered in early spring and boiled for a good hour or longer before leaving to cool; other ingredients are added such as lemon, ginger and brown sugar. Given that most recipes use large quantities of nettle, there might be some truth to the belief that nettle beer was an exceptionally strengthening and nutritious spring tonic – particularly after a lack of sunshine and meagre diets over winter.

In East Anglia, nettle beer was considered to be a primary medicinal beer of the region and in Lincolnshire it was recommended for tuberculosis.

Stephen Harrod Buhner (1998) found that drinking nettle beer alleviated arthritis in his hands – surely a more pleasant remedy than thrashing oneself with nettles:

> "Having suffered from arthritic conditions in my hands from years of using hammers and typewriters, I have found a periodic use of nettles in this manner (every five years or so) alleviates all the symptoms I have suffered. When made into beer or tea, the fluids contained in the fresh stinging hairs dissolve in the water, and when consumed produce the same effects."

Aside from the beverage's obvious health benefits, Buhner, one suspects, is a connoisseur of nettle beer. "The taste really is indescribable, being a blend of a number of flavours, a veritable gustatory extravaganza."

Given its past popularity as a wholesome green and a delicious drink, will nettle ever return to our kitchens as a culinary delicacy? Around the world the wild herb is used to create various culinary sensations. In 2012 John Lewis-Stempel recommended nettle puree spread on toast, topped with a poached egg. In Turkey nettle is known as a common wild edible green, and in Croatia it's sold in the vegetable markets of Dalmatia.

North American herbals suggest nettle is an excellent staple and among the best wild vegetables, with an exquisite taste. The raw, young leaves can be added to salads or cooked as greens in all types of dishes – sweet and savoury – or made into soup.

In South Africa the Sotho and Zulu add cooked salted nettle leaves as a relish and the Lovedu use nettle leaves like spinach; in the Stutterheim district of the Cape, boiled nettle tops are mixed with meal to make a paste, and in Lesotho young nettles are eaten as pot herbs. The stinging plant is also a good substitute for pepper due to its burning taste.

If you feel inspired to gather nettle and cook it at home, however, do take heed of Pliny's warning, should you also choose to raise geese – for the plant is said to be fatal to goslings.

RECIPES

Creamed Nettles

- 4 handfuls of nettles (chopped finely)
- 25g butter
- 25g plain flour
- 600ml milk
- 2tbsp crème fraîche
- 2tbsp natural yoghurt
- 2tbsp parmesan cheese (grated)
- ¼tsp nutmeg (freshly grated)
- salt and pepper to taste

Melt butter in a saucepan on a medium heat. Stir in the flour and cook for 1 minute. Take the pan off the heat, and slowly add the milk stirring all the time. If you don't you'll end up with lumps, not a problem but everyone and their granny will know you're a crap cook. Next stir in the nettles and return the pan to the heat and simmer stirring continuously for about 5 minutes until the sauce thickens up. Now add the crème fraîche, yoghurt, parmesan cheese, nutmeg, salt and pepper and stir them all in as well. Cook for another 1-2 minutes, then serve. Serves 3.

Nettle and Barley Risotto

- 80g nettles
- 70g wild garlic (chopped)
- 3g dried kelp
- 200g pearl barley
- 500ml stock
- 200ml nettle & kelp water
- 40g parmesan cheese
- 2tbsp cream cheese
- 1 onion
- 3 garlic cloves (chopped)
- 3 tbsp of vegetable oil
- black pepper

Put nettles and kelp into a pan and cover with water. Bring to a simmer and cook for 10 minutes. Drain, reserving the liquid. Remove the kelp, and squeeze the nettles to remove any excess liquid, then chop. In a large frying pan or paella dish add 2 tablespoons of oil, and gently fry the onion for about 3 minutes until soft and translucent, next add the garlic and stir so as not to burn it.

Add another tablespoon of oil, then pour in the barley, add the chopped nettles and stir to coat. Mix together 500ml of stock (I use a good chicken stock) with 200ml of the reserved nettle/kelp liquid, called from now on simply; the stock

Add a ladle of the stock, and stir continuously until it has been absorbed by the barley. Keep ladling the stock in small amounts until the barley is cooked. When you have only about 200ml left of the stock add in the chopped wild garlic. Remember to keep stirring all the time, so the barley doesn't burn. When the barley is cooked, add the parmesan cheese, cream cheese and black pepper. Stir together and serve. Serves 2.

Nettle Cordial

- 200g freshly picked nettle tops
- 1kg granulated sugar
- 40g citric acid (32 tbsp lemon juice).
- 500ml water
- Sterile glass bottles with tops, either screw or cork

Collect, wash and spin dry in a salad spinner 200g of nettle tops. Weigh out 1kg of granulated sugar. Measure out 40g of citric acid. Citric acid can often be found in health shops or home brewing shops. Add the granulated sugar, citric acid and water to a large saucepan, and heat the mixture until it reaches 60 degrees C, then remove from the heat. Now add the Nettle leaves, and stir well so that they get covered with the liquid, then cover and leave for a week. Make sure that you stir your mixture daily. After a week is up, sterilise your bottles, then strain the liquid through a sieve or colander and bottle. After opening a bottle, make sure that you refrigerate.

MEDICINE

The employment of nettle in folk remedies dates back over two thousand years. It appears as a remedy in ancient Egyptian writings, it's among the healing herbs of the Bible, and it was widely used by the ancient Greeks and Romans. The plant was listed in the works of Theophrastus, Pliny and Hippocrates.

Of course, magic and healing went hand in hand in early medicine. A love charm for divination became a helpful herb for fertility. The Romans would brush the genitals of a 'frigid' woman or an animal refusing to be serviced with nettles to stimulate sexual drive, though it would seem to us today that this would have had the opposite effect. Roman writer Caius Petronius claimed a man's virility was similarly improved if he was whipped with nettles below the belly button.

Nettle root was believed to promote love if dug up on St John's Day and placed on an altar, while saying 'Hail Mary' three times; the root supposedly stimulated pregnancy too. In Greece, the seeds were used as an aphrodisiac. In parts of Europe, if a girl was considered to be a nymphomaniac, it was said: "The daughter has urinated in the nettles" (de Cleene and Lejeune, 2003).

Not all accounts supported nettle's reputation as an aphrodisiac.

> "There is one record, from a New Forest gypsy in 1952, of nettles being used as a contraceptive. A man should lay nettle leaves thickly as a sole inside his socks and wear them for 24 hours before engaging in intercourse. The gypsy claimed to have tried this, and proved its effectiveness."
>
> — VICKERY, 1997

Centuries earlier, King Henry VIII's physician Andrew Borde had a similar idea about the plant. He wrote that "nettles in the cold pece" was a good remedy for married men who desired other women. It's doubtful that Henry VIII followed his doctor's advice (Michael, 2007).

From the fires of passion to the fires of healing, in the Doctrine of Signatures, a fiery (stinging) plant like nettle could cure burning conditions of the body and soul. Thus, a person suffering from nettle rash, other skin rashes or eczema, or who was feeling irritable, could drink a decoction of nettles to feel better.

Fighting fire with fire, Grieve (1931) wrote that cloths soaked in nettle tincture or a nettle ointment could heal burns.

Nettle was purported to cure a fever, thanks to its fiery nature. In Germany, treatment involved either the leaves, the roots (sprinkled with salt and a spell), or the plant itself, simply left to wither on the patient. Culpeper (1653) praised the nettle's hot qualities as being good for warming a spring cold, among other things:

> "You know Mars is hot and dry, and you know as well that Winter is cold and moist; then you may know as well the reason why Nettle-tops eaten in the Spring consume the phlegmatic superfluities in the body of man, that the coldness and moistness of Winter hath left behind."

In Guernsey in the British Channels Isles, a liniment made from nettles, salt and oil was used by fisherman as a protection against the cold; it was rubbed on the spine, soles of the feet and wrists.

Pliny the Elder wrote about the roots of another species of nettle – the autumn nettle (*Autumnalis urtica*) – which he claimed could cure a person of their fever if the person's name was said, along with the name of their father, when the nettle was dug up.

Herbalist Catherine Oswald prescribed picking nettle by its root "three successive mornings before sunrise" to cure "trembling fever" (or ague) (Folkard, 1892).

Nettle's 'warming' quality made it a popular treatment for rheumatism and other ailments, such as dropsy, paralysis, lumbago and sciatica, that could benefit from rubbing a stinging plant on the body to stimulate circulation and create 'warmth'. In Ireland nettle plants picked from a churchyard and boiled down were used to treat dropsy (an excessive accumulation of fluids in the body), and in Russian folk medicine an infusion of the roots was used instead. Ancient Egyptians also applied an infusion of nettle to relieve arthritis and lumbago.

Roman soldiers famously rubbed their bodies with nettle to promote good circulation and to stay warm. In cold, damp Britain, the troops also beat themselves with nettle to help alleviate rheumatic joints. It's not clear whether the stinging nettle (*Urtica dioica*) that we know today was the same nettle used by the Romans for self-flagellation. Richard Folkard (1892) suggested it was the Roman nettle (*Urtica pilulifera*) that was brought to Britain with the Roman armies and which is the "most venomous of British nettles," found abundantly in Kent. He wrote:

> "According to Camden, the Roman soldiers brought the seed with them, and sowed it for their own use, to rub and chafe their limbs when, through extreme cold, they should be stiff and benumbed; having been told before they came from home that the climate of England was so cold that it was not to be endured without having recourse to some friction to warm their blood and to stir up natural heat."

By 1794, self-flagellating with nettles had become the "time-honoured tradition" for stimulating and restoring paralysed limbs (de Cleene and Lejeune, 2015). Grieve wrote that flogging with nettle to treat ailments such as rheumatism was known as 'urtication'. However, in some places people would lie down in nettles to get stung and allow the ailment, or the evil, to leave the body in the blisters.

While urtication seems like an archaic method for treating rheumatism today, there is some method in the madness. Stephen Harrod Buhner (1998) explained that the stinging hairs of nettle act like miniature needles when broken and 'inject' a fluid containing histamines, acetylcholine and formic acid just under the surface of the skin. These components play an important role in the transmission of nerves, which might be useful in treating arthritic conditions. He compared the use of nettles for rheumatism to naturopathic treatments using bee stings, which also contain acetylcholine, although nettles are probably safer to use and don't involve killing a bee.

Gerard (1597) added to nettle's stinging virtues by writing that it makes "the vital spirit more lively".

Hildegard commented on nettle's 'warm type' being good for purging mucus from the stomach and prescribed it: "[should] worms grow up from the harmful and bad humors that are poisonous in the person". The herbalist also suggested anointing a person on the chest and temples with a juice of nettles to dispel forgetfulness.

In ancient times when death by poisoning was perhaps more common, or when it was a popular method of assassination, antidotes to poisons often featured in medical manuscripts. Ancient writers like Theophrastus, Dioscorides and Pliny also prescribed nettle for various ailments – sprains, nosebleeds, colds, abscesses, gout and cancerous sores – and as an antidote for poisoning by certain other plants, as well as bites and stings inflicted by dogs, salamanders, snakes, and scorpions. Apollodorus, a student of Hippocrates (c460–c377 BC), boiled a broth of nettle and tortoise as an antidote to the bite of a salamander, and for the poison of henbane, serpents and scorpions. Gerard later wrote that nettle is an effective remedy for poisoning caused by hemlock, mushrooms and quicksilver (mercury).

So widely valued was nettle among early physicians that Hippocrates and his followers listed sixty-one medicinal uses for the plant. These included purging the uterus, to expel intestinal worms, for gout and other joint diseases, and to restore hair loss. Adding to Hippocrates' teachings, Galen later recommended nettle leaves as a diuretic and laxative, as well as for dog bites, gangrene, swelling, nosebleeds, relieving menstruation, for illnesses of the spleen, and for pleurisy, pneumonia, asthma, tinea and mouth sores. Clearly nettle was one of the cure-alls of the ancient world.

Another important use for nettle in traditional herbal medicine was as a blood tonic and astringent, as it was believed to purify or strengthen the blood and to staunch bleeding. The *Aztecs Herbal* of 1552 includes a remedy of crushed nettles in milk to stop nosebleeds, and prescribes a nettle poultice for arthritis. Pechey (1694) wrote that nettle was notable for its blood staunching properties and for stopping a nosebleed. Grieve noted nettle was used as "an arrester of bleeding" from the nose, lungs or stomach when applied as a tincture or taken internally as a fresh herb.

Nettle's use as a vulnerary herb continued in more recent herbal medicine, with descriptions of crushed nettles being used to staunch nosebleeds, or nettle tea being drunk to purify the blood (in Belgium). The herb also remained popular for treating heavy menstrual bleeding and anaemia, among many other conditions including haemorrhoids, bronchitis, boils and skin complaints, measles and rashes, rheumatism, paralysed limbs, circulatory problems, epilepsy, and poor digestion.

In medieval times, nettle was one of the ingredients used in a remedy for shingles. The patient was required to drink the remedy for ten nights, and then to drink mistletoe (now known to be poisonous) in wine for nine days, without eating any meat. Soothing salves were made with nettle and other plants to apply externally. Medieval physicians also prescribed nettle for a plethora of other conditions from constipation to sinusitis.

Home uses for nettle involved treating coughs, colds and chest complaints. Gerard noted it was useful for whooping cough in children. In Russian folk medicine, nettle tea was helpful for asthma. In the Scottish Highlands, nettle roots were a remedy for consumption (tuberculosis). In England the seeds were used (Somerset) or a nettle beer was drunk (East Anglia); and smoke from burning nettles was said to be good for the chest.

Nettle was recommended for treating problems in the lungs and kidneys by Salmon in 1693 and Pechey in 1694, and its use to treat lung complaints was later supported by Grieve in her work *A Modern Herbal* (1931), who recommended it for asthma, although she doubted its use as a diuretic for alleviating kidney problems.

A list of thirty to forty ailments that could be treated by nettle was given by William Coles, along with the suggestion that the herb could foretell the outcome of a patient. If a nettle put in a pot of the patient's urine was fresh and green a day later, the patient would live, but if not it would signify death or danger.

In Wales, nettle broth was used to stimulate appetite and to promote sleep, while a Welsh legend said that "eating nettles in spring would cultivate a good memory" (Watts, 2007).

In the eighteenth century, nettle juice was dripped into the ear for earache, and chopped nettles in egg white were rubbed on the temples for insomnia. Elizabeth Blackwell's *Curious Herbal* noted nettle's application for nosebleeds, wounds, as a diuretic, for jaundice, coughs and shortness of breath. The preacher John Wesley, in his work *Primitive Physic*, wrote that nettle was a good treatment for bleeding wounds, internal bleeding, pleurisy, worms, sciatica and as a cure for nettle rash.

By the nineteenth century, nettle was still used for a large number of conditions. In fact, its use seemed to grow from era to era. Physicians of the nineteenth century recommended nettle for scurvy, tuberculosis, rheumatism, urinary and kidney disease, and even in large doses for cancer. Thornton's nineteenth-century *Family Herbal* prescribed nettle for treating anything from cancers and paralysed limbs to nosebleeds and scurvy. In the Norfolk Fens in England, nettle leaves, followed by dock leaves, were rubbed on a patient suffering from smallpox. This continued up until the late nineteenth century.

Around the world it seemed there was nothing nettle couldn't cure. In Ireland, nettles were used to treat sores, rashes, eczema, boils, various infections, colds, coughs, rheumatism, to purify the blood, rid the body of worms (particularly in the case of children), dropsy and jaundice; and it was apparently the best cure for measles.

In Russia, nettle leaves were an ingredient in a medicine for chronic hepatitis, cholangitis, cholecystitis and constipation, being considered "powerfully diuretic".

In the *King's America Dispensatory* of the 1800s, which lists plants in America used in a branch of medicine known as 'Eclectic', nettle is recommended as a diuretic for treating cystitis and urinary incontinence. The Eclectics claimed the plant was astringent and haemostatic, and useful for eczema, diarrhoea and haemorrhoids. In Native American traditions, pregnant women drank nettle tea as a strengthening tonic for their uterus, blood and unborn babies.

Among India's documented lists of useful plants, nettle is used from root to tip. The roots and seeds can treat diarrhoea and worms, and the leaves and roots are good for dandruff and hair growth.

In Nepal, the uses of nettle differ from village to village. A root decoction treats asthma in many places. The root is chewed for dental cavities in Jajarkot and a paste of the root is applied to dog bites. The Tamangs of Sindhupalchok add sparrow and rat droppings to nettle root paste to treat cuts and wounds, whereas the Tharus of Dangdeokhuri apply the plain paste. Danuwars and Magars use nettle root paste with another herb to reset dislocated bones. The Rautes drink nettle juice for bile disease. In eastern Nepal, villagers eat nettle leaves for coughs and colds, and apply a paste of the fruits for dislocated bones.

In Morocco all parts of the plant are used in traditional herbal medicine: internally as a remedy for headaches, chills, tuberculosis, spleen and kidney disorders, and externally for skin problems, scabies, pruritus and haemorrhoids.

Stinging nettles are still widely employed as medicinal plants in the Mediterranean in herbal remedies for poor circulation, urinary, digestive and respiratory disorders, and externally for dandruff and alopecia.

Nettle is widely available to buy in health food stores as a tea or dried herb. Today's herbalists might recommend its use for regulating menstrual cycles; as a detoxifying tonic; as a diuretic; or for treating anaemia, diarrhoea, gout, rheumatism and arthritis, skin problems or hair loss. Some herbals record its use for improving liver and kidney function, jaundice, ulcers, haemorrhoids, asthma and bronchitis.

The plant is not listed in the *British Pharmacopoeia*, although its use is still widespread in herbal medicine.

Nettle can be used as a simple home remedy, for instance taken from spring to autumn for hayfever and similar allergies. Nettle has long been a traditional treatment for improving the condition of hair; Grieve suggested rinsing with nettle tonic every other night to stop hair falling out and to make it soft. Today nettle is sometimes used as an ingredient of commercially produced shampoos and conditioners.

Nettle tea is considered an excellent drink for recuperating from illness, injury or surgery, being rich in vitamins and minerals. Nettle seeds too are considered helpful for exhaustion: "In the early twentieth century, a German naturopath used the trick in a home for the elderly. The residents got a tablespoon of nettle seeds each day. Sure enough, they got a spring in their step, a love of life—and a love life" (Kress, 2011). A recent study in the *Journal of The American Herbalist Guild* found that nettle seed improved kidney function, and modern herbalists report that patients with kidney problems have benefited from taking nettle seed.

Today more is known about nettle's chemistry and how it works. Among its notable constituents are caffeic and malic acids, which are thought to be anti-inflammatory. Paine (2006) wrote that nettle leaf extract is documented in *The Complete German Commission E Monographs*, to be prescribed for rheumatism, and that research had been conducted on its anti-inflammatory component, caffeic acid.

Recent studies seem to support traditional uses for nettle in food and medicine, with findings suggesting that the plant is highly nutritious and has a promising potential for future pharmaceuticals.

A study led by Yunuskhodzhaeva (2014) concluded that nettle is a promising source for pharmacologically active substances. Joshi and team (2014) conducted a review of nettle's pharmacological properties and found that various biological properties supported its use in some ailments. While many useful components were identified, the authors of the study concluded there is more scope for research. Similarly, Asgarpanah and Mohajerani (2012) researched the phytochemical and pharmacologic properties of stinging nettle. They found potential to explore the plant as a therapeutic agent in the development of new drugs, although they were cautious that further research was needed into its effectiveness and safety.

Ghaima and team (2013) compared the chemical activity of nettle and Dandelion, and found nettle has more effective antibacterial and antioxidant activities than Dandelion. Zeipina's team (2015) discovered that antioxidant activity in nettle leaves varies at different stages of the plant's development. Bourgeois and team (2016) studied nettle for its anti-aging applications in cosmetics; they confirmed that certain nettle extracts displayed a strong antioxidant potential, which could be of interest to the cosmetic industry.

Adhikari and team (2015) compared the nutritional properties of stinging nettle flour with wheat and barley flours. They established that nettle compared favourably with wheat and barley, with a higher content of certain nutrients such as protein, fibre, calcium and iron. In addition, they supported stinging nettle's medicinal value in the relief of arthritis, rheumatism and muscular pain.

The European Medicines Agency's assessment report on *Urtica dioica* (2010) concluded that the traditional use of nettle leaf for minor joint pain and for minor urinary complaints was supported by pharmacological research. In addition, nettle did not carry the same side effects as pharmaceutical anti-inflammatory drugs, which could cause serious gastrointestinal irritation and have cardiovascular risks if taken in excess.

Research by Guil-Guerrero and team (2002) showed nettle leaf was a good source of essential fatty acids and other nutrients, which could be considered part of a healthy diet for humans.

Rutto and team (2013) looked at the nutritional values of raw and processed stinging nettles. Their results showed that 100g of processed nettle supplies high amounts (90 to 100%) of vitamin A and is rich in calcium, iron and protein. They recommended fresh or processed nettle as a high-protein, nutritious and low-calorie food source in specialised diets such as for vegetarians or diabetics.

Belščak-Cvitanović and team (2015) evaluated chocolates enriched with nettle extract and compared their nutritional content and flavour upon production and after twelve months in storage. Overall, they found the nutritional quality and taste of chocolate containing freeze-dried nettle extract performed well after storage. Despite its proven nutritional value, nettle remains an underused ingredient of the food industry.

Sanderson and Predergast (2012) looked at commercial uses of nettle and found only three enterprises that exploited the plant as a food source. These were: nettle wrapping for Yarg cheese produced by Lynher Farms and Dairies in Liskeard, Cornwall; a leaf curd product made by Leafcycle in Tiverton, Devon; and a nettle cordial and sparkling drink manufactured by Thorncroft in Stockton, Cleveland.

According to Paine (2006), the most promising research on nettle involves investigation into its plant lectins which, among other things, can improve symptoms of an enlarged prostate in men.

Research into these plant lectins was carried out by Peuman and team (1983), who found that they stimulated the immune system. Further research identified that lectins had antifungal properties for plants and that they inhibited autoimmune diseases in mice. It was Hyrb and team (1995) who found that nettle root extracts could help to improve symptoms of an enlarged prostate in men. A continuation of this research in the 1990s found nettle root extract improved urinary flow in patients with an enlarged prostate, and in 1996 nettle root extract was approved for treating prostatic diseases in Germany. Scientists found that nettle root compared favourably with the pharmaceutical drug Finasteride, prescribed for enlarged prostate, but with fewer side effects; for instance, there were fewer cases of erectile dysfunction and headaches. Of course, it's advised that using nettle for prostate problems is only done under proper medical supervision.

SAFETY NOTE

Nettle's most notorious unpleasant effect is its stinging hairs, which may cause rare allergic reactions (hives, itching, swelling) in some people. There are some recorded cases of nettle tea causing digestive irritation, and several examples of warnings not to pick the older plants in summer or autumn, because eating these in larger quantities might cause kidney problems.

Today's texts on herbal medicine sometimes list nettle as contraindicated for those who have high or low blood pressure, for people taking anti-depressants, and for diabetics.

While few drug interactions are known, it's advised not to take nettle with digitalis. In fact, research to support many of the safety precautions for nettle is not wholly conclusive, but it may be wise to take heed of them. Modern herbals vary in their advice to pregnant and breastfeeding women, but it's always best to err on the side of caution.

BOTANICAL PROFILE

Scientific Name: *Urtica dioica.*

Family: Urticaceae.

Botanical Description

Height: around 1–2.5 m. Growth: spread up to 850 m. Flowers: small, green, catkin-like flowers with no petals. Leaves and stem: dull green, serrated and covered all over in stinging hairs; toothy, heart-shaped leaves. Fruit: flowers ripen into tiny, flat, seed-like nuts.

Flowers: May to September.

Status: Perennial. Native.

Habitat: Deciduous woodland, coniferous woodland, cultivated land, grassland, hedgerows, meadow, mountains, river banks, roadsides, scrub, wasteland.

Stinging Nettle (*Urtica dioica*)

15
SWEET VIOLET

There are around four hundred species of violet found in the world, many of which are economically important. Three species of violets in particular are considered here – *Viola odorata*, *Viola riviniana*, and *Viola tricolor* – all of which have a collection of popular European names. For example, the common names of Wild Pansy (*V. tricolor*) often refer to the resemblance of the flower to a face or figure, such as 'cat's faces' and 'monkey's face'.

With so many species to distinguish between and so many popular names to identify them, in literature there is often much confusion around the description of violet. For instance, the purple-coloured varieties of the flower can be distinguished from the rest by the Greek name 'Ion', "from which the purple colour ianthine is derived", wrote Marcel de Cleene and Marie Claire Lejeune (2003). Another explanation for the 'io' in the word 'violet' is that it comes from the name 'Io', the lover of Zeus, or Jupiter, in Greek myth. The king of the gods changed Io into a cow to hide her from his jealous wife Hera, or Juno, and then created violets as food for the cow. For this reason, the violet is sometimes known in Flemish as Jupiterbloem or 'Jupiter's flower'.

Geoffrey Grigson (1996) suggested that what really pulled the violet out of obscurity was its scent. He wrote: "Scent suggested sex, so the violet was a flower of Aphrodite and also of her son Priapus, the deity of gardens and generation ... A flower so deeply and finely scented must also have its virtues in physic."

FOOD

Sweet Violet, *V. odorata* is one of the most economically important species of violet, wrote Peter Wyse Jackson (2014). It is grown commercially in southern France for the production of essential oils in the manufacture of perfume, flavouring and cosmetics. Around 100 g of flowers are used to produce 31 g of essential oil of violet by a process of macerating the petals in hot fat, and about 1000 g of violet leaves are used to produce 400 g of violet absolute (Uphof, 1959). The absolute and essential oil have a wide variety of uses in perfumes and cosmetics for hair and skin.

Sweet Violet is also used to produce a sweet liqueur called *'parfait amour'*, and the Persians and Romans appreciated a wine made from fragrant violets. A wreath of violets was used by Romans to cure hangovers, and the Greeks and Romans used violets to flavour butter, oil, vinegar and wine. In fact, violets were one of the first flowers grown commercially in Greece, around 300–400 BC.

Violet flowers can also be crystallised and used as edible decorations. The practice of pairing violets with sugar has existed since the Middle Ages in recipes for caudle sugar (blue violet sugar) and violet syrup. A medieval recipe for a popular pudding called 'Mon Amy' was made with violet syrup. According to Mrs Grieve (1931), in the recipe for Mon Amy, the cook was instructed to "plant it with flowers of violet and serve forth". In the fourteenth century, violets were mixed with ground almonds and cream in the making of a rice pudding.

The Tudors enjoyed violet syrups and conserves, and ate the leaves with salads and pottages. The leaves were used in Elizabethan salads known as Grand Salletts. Violets continued to be a favourite among royalty even up to Victorian times. John Evelyn described an "agreeable herbaceous dish" of violet leaves fried and eaten with lemon or orange juice and sugar. Today an extract of the leaf is used for flavouring ice creams, candies and baked goods. Violets have been used to flavour sherbet in Asia Minor and the Middle East, have been served at banquets since ancient times, and have even flavoured the national drink of Syria and Turkey.

Like many wildflowers, violets were countryside snacks not so long ago. Roy Vickery has provided an account from Devon in 1993: "I was born in 1914. This area was then pure farming. Occasionally we would eat violet seeds – not the green pod – when they were white".

Violets still have appeal in cooking, simply for their appearance. The flowers make a pretty garnish sprinkled over salads, omelettes, cakes and desserts. De Cleene and Lejeune wrote that wild pansies are not suitable for most recipes, because of their unpleasant taste, whereas the larger fragrant violets are a good choice for most flower dishes. They wrote: "In gastronomic restaurants, violet water is used to scent dishes." The flower has been the guest star of celebrity chefs, wrote TK Lim (2012): "In the recent Chelsea Flower Show, top chef Marcus Wareing used Sweet Violet flowers to garnish his gin and tonic granita, an unusual take on the famous English tipple". If you fancy something simpler, violet tea is easily made by pouring hot water over the petals or flower heads, and is just as likely to impress at tea parties.

Twentieth-century herbalists like Eleanour Sinclair Rohde (1969) provided many delicious recipes for violets, explaining how to make violet syrup, violet honey and flower-inspired conserves and cakes. Rohde also provided a method for making traditional violet tablets and vinegars, as prescribed by the likes of Pliny and Gerard.

Less traditional suggestions for violet that provide a modern culinary twist include adding the chopped leaves to salads and soups, or dipping a leaf in batter and frying as an appetizer. The leaves make a tasty sandwich in bread and butter.

Violet leaves may complement other wild edibles such as wild okra and dock, or make an aromatic addition to lamb dishes. They have also been used as elaborate floral dressings for joints of veal. Larger leaves can be used to wrap tofu, rice, potatoes or beans. The stems can be chopped and lightly cooked as 'beans', and served as a side dish to many meals.

The leaves of various North American species of violets were used by people to thicken soups. In Asia, violet leaves are cooked as greens. Different species of violet have been listed as a wild vegetable and a spice or seasoning in countries such as Bosnia and the Czech Republic. In Italy, violets are grown as a culinary herb.

Nutritionally, violet leaves are high in vitamin C as well as containing vitamin A and various other minerals and saponins. Research suggests the plant also has significant antioxidant activity. Mrs Grieve reminds us that all recipes using violet not only benefit from the flower's aroma, flavour and nutritious qualities, but also from its rich colour. Violet vinegar, for example, will have a brilliant tint.

RECIPES

Fried Violet Leaves

Fry violet leaves in butter until they start turning brown, then add orange or lemon juice and a sprinkling of sugar.

Traditional Violet Syrup

- 50g Sweet Violet flowers
- 150ml boiling water
- 300g caster sugar

Put the violet flowers into a bowl that is small enough to fit inside large saucepan (bain-marie) and pour boiling water over them. Allow to infuse over night. In the morning put the bowl of water and flowers inside a large saucepan. Fill the saucepan with water but make sure it doesn't go into the bowl of flowers. Next add the caster sugar to the bowl of flowers then heat the saucepan and stir the bowl of flowers until the sugar has all dissolved. Strain the violet mixture through a fine sieve layered with muslin and bottle in sterilised bottles and cap. Store in a cool, dark cupboard.

Violet Jam

- 1 pack of Kraft Sure Jell (or other pectin)
- 2½ cups of water
- ½ cup of lemon juice
- 3 cups of sugar
- 1 cup of violet flowers

Mix the pectin, water and lemon juice together, then bring to a boil, add the sugar and simmer for 3 minutes. Remove from the heat, add the Violet flowers and stir them in. Allow to infuse for 60 minutes then pour into sterilised jars and cap.

MEDICINE

For a magical healer, violets could be used to cure all manner of supernatural maladies. The ancient Greeks wore violet wreaths to induce sleep, to calm anger and to cheer the heart. Like many spring plants, the first violets to appear were thought to be the most potent and could be used to ensure a person would have no illness for a whole year. A belief in Germany was that stroking your eyes with the first three violets of the year protected against the Evil Eye. A sixteenth-century collection of remedies from Brussels told of the special healing properties of the first spring violets: "In order not to lose your strength. If you see a violet, pick the flower using your middle finger and greedily eat one flower, followed by a second and a third. The number of years you have done this equals the number of years you will not be sick" (translated; de Cleene and Lejeune, 2003).

More medicine than magic, the violet was included by Greek physicians such as Hippocrates, Theophrastus and Dioscorides in remedies for eyes and throat, and for convulsions. Rome's Pliny the Elder (c77 AD) wrote that purple violets were 'cooling', and also recommended them for the eyes and throat, as well as for burning headaches and lumps on the buttocks or womb. Pliny said that violets should be used dried for medicinal purposes, and gathered one year before use for the most powerful effects. Other remedy recipes in antiquity for the plant used the leaves mixed with honey for headaches, mixed with wax for healing cracks in the anus, and mixed with vinegar to cure abscesses or gout. The ancients also used strongly scented 'violet balls', made from Sweet Violets, to revive people who had fainted.

The folk uses of violet were similar to those used by the ancients. For example, in Irish folk medicine, *V. odorata* was once used to treat tumours and headaches. In his sixteenth-century herbal, John Gerard wrote about violets:

> "The floures are good for all inflammation, especially of the sides and lungs; they take away the hoarseness of the chest, the rugedness of the winde-pipe and jaws, and take away the thirst. There is likewise made of Violets and sugar certain plates called Sugar Violet, or Violet tables, or Plate, which is most pleasant and wholesome, especially it comforteth the heart and the other inward parts."

Culpeper, like Pliny, praised violets for their cooling effects and ability to heal inflammation in the body, particularly in the case of the eyes and the head. He wrote in 1653: "They are a fine pleasing plant of Venus, of a mild nature, no way harmful." Culpeper prescribed violets for insomnia, lung diseases, liver problems, urinary complaints and jaundice, among various other conditions. Of the wild pansy, Culpeper referred to the flower as a "really saturnine" herb. He particularly recommended the plant as a treatment for the "French pox", or syphilis.

Hildegard of Bingen judged the violet to be between hot and cold, and especially praised the flower as a remedy for the eyes:

> "It is useful for cloudy eyes. Take good oil and make it hot either in the sun or in a fire in a new pot … At night put this oil around the eyelids and eyes, but do not let it touch the eye itself; the cloudiness will flee from the eyes."

The Sweet Violet was particularly popular in European folk medicine. A Flemish remedy involved infusing violets overnight, then heating with sugar to make a syrup. This was used as a laxative, expectorant and treatment for thrush. A Slovakian remedy involved macerating the blue petals of Sweet Violet in oil and sunlight for thirty days, then filtering through a cloth and bottling as healing oil of violet. *A Book of Fruits and Flowers*, written by Thomas Jenner in 1663, mentions various uses for violet oil – from curing headaches and sleeplessness to relieving melancholy and "heaviness of spirit".

Violets steeped in goat's milk were used as a cosmetic remedy by ancient Britons to enhance a woman's beauty. The Saxons recommended the herb as an internal remedy for wounds; although it was also known to rid a person of afflictions caused by evil spirits. In later British folk medicine, violets were drunk in an infusion or used externally as a poultice to treat cancerous tumours. A gypsy remedy for cancerous growths used an infusion of violet leaves. In fact David Allen and Gabrielle Hatfield (2004) wrote on this point:

> "The most widespread folk application of violets has been for cancerous tumours, either on their own or in combination with other herbs, either externally or internally, either by crushing the fresh leaves and laying them on as a poultice or eating them or drinking an infusion."

De Cleene and Lejeune tell us that oil of violets remains a popular remedy in contemporary herbals for headaches and fever, while Le Strange wrote that violets were once included in the pharmacopoeias of the US for various uses including bronchitis, asthma and catarrh. The syrup of Sweet Violet may be used to treat colds and bronchitis.

Present-day herbal medicine makes particular use of the plant's roots because of their expectorant and stimulating effects, which are beneficial for coughs, colds, bronchitis and sore throats. The expectorant leaves and flowers of *V. tricolor* might also be taken for similar ailments. The root is also used to make eyewashes, mouthwashes and to treat thrush. Violets are considered by several sources to be an emetic.

Fresh violet petals can be made into a poultice to treat cracked, sore nipples. An infusion of the flowers is thought to have laxative effects, while also providing a soothing and disinfecting flower water tonic. The seeds are thought to be purgative and diuretic.

Modern herbalists regard the leaves of violet as being antiseptic; they can be taken internally as a tea or applied externally as a compress. Violet leaf tea, or a decoction of the leaves, is said to be good for coughs. In Ecuador, violet teas are particularly valued for medicinal purposes.

The pain-relieving actions of violet in treating conditions such as headaches and coughs, and its soothing effects for treating insomnia, are thought to be due to the plant's salicylic acid content.

Duke (2002) recommended violet for a range of uses both related to and other than those listed above, including stomach ache, heart palpitations and nervousness.

While plant cousins often have similar uses in plant medicine, it seems some species of violet have particular uses. Le Strange wrote that *V. tricolor* has been used in a homeopathic tincture for skin complaints and weakness of the heart. Other sources say the flower can be used in homeopathy for eye diseases and earache. The leaves are also thought to be a remedy for epilepsy and infant diseases. *V. odorata* is thought to be especially good for skin diseases, and may be why it is added, as an essential oil, to toiletries. Both the flowers and leaves are considered emollient, which is beneficial to skin.

In Chinese medicine, violet leaf and root poultices are used on hot swellings, inflammation and mumps.

Following in the footsteps of Culpeper, Bartram (2002) reports that *V. tricolor* has been used by "Dr Schlegel, Moscow, for sexually transmitted diseases generally, with ulceration". Also continuing ancient traditions, some modern herbals prescribe *V. odorata* taken with honey for headaches and coughs.

Modern sources also still recommend violets for cancerous growths. Bartram wrote:

> "When the wife of General Booth, Salvation Army Chief, was dying of cancer the one drink that gave her relief from the pain was Violet leaf tea [*V. odorata*] made from leaves foraged from railway embankments by devoted members of the Army."

Herbalpedia suggests violet's blood purifying properties are connected to its use as a treatment for cancer. Some research also suggests the plant can prevent the haemorrhaging of capillaries; it is the plant's constituent rutin that helps to strengthen capillary walls, thus providing this protective action.

SAFETY NOTE

Several sources suggest that overuse of violet can be harmful, so it is a herb to use in moderation. Side effects may include vomiting. In addition, it's thought best to avoid using violet during pregnancy and when breastfeeding.

BOTANICAL PROFILE

Scientific Name: *Viola odorata.*

Family: Violaceae.

Botanical Description

Flowers: Five free petals, the lower one with a backward-pointing spur. Leaves: heart-shaped and serrated in varying sizes. Stems: Long, straggling stems.

Flowers: February to May.

Status: Perennial. Native.

Habitat: Deciduous woodland, hedgerows, scrub.

Sweet Violet (*Viola odorata*)

CONTINUE THE JOURNEY

'Just wanted to say, I think this is possibly the most beautiful newsletter I have ever received.'

— KATE NICHOLSON

Foraging can be a deep journey into Self. A gentle way to 'get out of your head and come to your senses.'

A way to experience the world and the plant kingdom through new eyes. A wondrous journey into wildness that comes from walking the Green Path.

Foraging reawakens your senses and helps you gain a greater appreciation of Nature and your place in the natural cycles and rhythms of life.

In the Eatweeds Newsletter, I share my wealth of knowledge on the past and present uses of wild plants as food and medicine.

As well as the importance of embodied nature-based practices to restore vital connection back to the living earth.

Welcome to the beautiful, mysterious world of plants.

Subscribe free at → www.eatweeds.co.uk/subscribe

ABOUT THE AUTHOR

Robin Harford is a plant forager, ethnobotanical researcher and wild food educator. He has published numerous foraging guide books.

He established his wild food foraging school in 2008, and his foraging courses were recently voted #1 in the country by BBC Countryfile.

Robin is the creator of eatweeds.co.uk, which is listed in The Times Top 50 websites for food and drink.

He has travelled extensively documenting and recording the traditional and local uses of wild food plants in indigenous cultures, and his work has taken him to Africa, India, SE Asia, Europe and the USA.

Robin occasionally appears on national and local radio and television. He has been recommended in BBC Good Food magazine, Sainsbury's magazine as well as in The Guardian, The Times, The Independent, The Daily Telegraph etc.

He is a member of the Society of Economic Botany and the Botanical Society of Britain and Ireland.

instagram.com/eatweedsuk
facebook.com/eatweedsuk

BIBLIOGRAPHY

Abbasi, A. M. et al. (2015) *Wild Edible Vegetables of Lesser Himalayas: Ethnobotanical and Nutraceutical Aspects, Volume 1.* Germany: Springer International Publishing.

Adhikari, B. M. et al. (2016) Comparison of Nutritional Properties of Stinging Nettle (Urtica dioica) Flour with Wheat and Barley Flours. *Food Science & Nutrition.* [Online] 4 (1), 119–124.

Akhtar, M. S. et al. (1985) Effects of Portulaca oleracae (kulfa) and Taraxacum officinale (dhudhal) in Normoglycaemic and Alloxan-Treated Hyperglycaemic Rabbits. *J Pak Med Assoc.* 35 (7), 207–210.

Allen, D. E. & Hatfield, G. (2004) *Medicinal Plants in Folk Tradition: An Ethnobotany of Britain & Ireland.* Portland: Timber Press.

Anon (2014) *Herbalpedia.*

Anon (1526) *The Grete Herball.* Peter Treveris.

Asgarpanah, J. & R, M. (2012) Phytochemistry and Pharmacologic Properties of Urtica dioica L. *Journal of Medicinal Plants Research.* 6.

Baker, M. (2008) *Discovering the Folklore of Plants*. Oxford: Shire Publications.

Bardswell, F. A. (1911) *The Herb-Garden*. A&C Black.

Barnes, J. et al. (2013) *Herbal Medicines*. 4. rev. ed. London: Pharmaceutical Press.

Belščak-Cvitanović, A. et al. (2015) Nettle (Urtica dioica L.) Extracts as Functional Ingredients for Production of Chocolates with Improved Bioactive Composition and Sensory Properties. *Journal of Food Science and Technology*. [Online] 52 (12), 7723–7734.

Bennet, S. (1991) *Food from Forests*. Dehradun, India: Indian Council of Forestry Research and Education.

Biancardi, E. et al. (2012) *Beta maritima: The Origin of Beets*. [Online]. New York: Springer-Verlag.

Bisht, S. et al. (n.d.) Urtica dioica (l): An Undervalued, Economically Important Plant. *Agricultural Science Research Journal*. 2 (5), 250–252.

Blackwell, E. et al. (1737) *A Curious Herbal Containing Five Hundred Cuts, of the Most Useful Plants, Which Are Now Used in the Practice of Physick Engraved on Folio Copper Plates, After Drawings Taken from the Life*. London: Printed for Samuel Harding,.

Blumenthal, M. (ed.) (2000) *The Complete German Commission E Monographs: Therapeutic Guide to Herbal Medicines*. Austin, Texas: Boston: Integrative Medicine.

Bonser, W. (1963) *The Medical Background of Anglo-Saxon England: A Study in History, Psychology, and Folklore*. London: Wellcome Historical Medical Library.

Bourgeois, C. et al. (2016) Nettle (Urtica dioica L.) as a Source of Antioxidant and Anti-Aging Phytochemicals for Cosmetic Applications. *Comptes Rendus Chimie*. [Online] 19 (9), 1090–1100.

Brinkkemper, O. (2015) Smyrnium olusatrum L. (alexanders): An Ancient Kitchen Herb from Late Medieval Rotterdam (the Netherlands). *Vegetation History and Archaeobotany*. [Online] 24 (1), 249–252.

Buhner, S. H. (1998) *Sacred and Herbal Healing Beers: The Secrets of Ancient Fermentation*. Boulder: Siris Books.

Burgess, J. T. (1868) *Old English Wild Flowers: To Be Found by the Wayside, Fields, Hedgerows, Rivers, Moorlands, Meadows, Mountains and Sea-Shore*. F. Warne & Company.

Caprioli, G. et al. (2014) Ascorbic Acid Content, Fatty Acid Composition and Nutritional Value of the Neglected Vegetable Alexanders (Smyrnium olusatrum L., Apiaceae). *Journal of Food Composition and Analysis*. [Online] 35 (1), 30–36.

Čeh, B. et al. (2013) Symposium Proceedings. New Challenges in Agronomy 2013, Zreče, Slovenia, 24-25 January, 2013. *Symposium Proceedings. New challenges in agronomy 2013, Zreče, Slovenia, 24-25 January, 2013*.

Chakarski, I. (1982) Clinical Study of a Herb Combination Consisting of Agrimonia eupatoria, Hipericum perforatum, Plantago major, Mentha piperita, Matricaria chamomila for the Treatment of Patients with Chronic Gastroduodenitis. *Probl Vatr Med*. 1078–84.

Civelek, C. & Balkaya, A. (2013) The Nutrient Content of Some Wild Plant Species Used as Vegetables in Bafra Plain Located in the Black Sea Region of Turkey. *The European Journal of Plant Science and Biotechnology*.

Cleene, M. de & Lejeune, M. C. (2002) *Compendium of Symbolic and Ritual Plants in Europe*. Ghent: Man & Culture.

Coles, W. (1657) *Adam in Eden, or, Natures Paradise: The History of Plants, Fruits, Herbs and Flowers: With Their Several Names, Whether Greek, Latin or English, the Places Where They Grow, Their Descriptions and Kinds, Their Times of Flourishing and Decreasing, as Also Their Several Signatures, Anatomical Appropriations, and Particular Physical Vertues, Together with Necessary Observations on the Seasons of Planting, and Gathering of Our English Simples with Directions How to Preserve Them in Their Compositions or Otherwise ... for the Herbalists Greater Benefit, There Is Annexed a Latin and English Table of the Several Names of Simples, with Another More Particular Table of the Diseases, and Their Cures, Treated of in This so Necessary a Work*. J. Streater.

Couplan, F. (1998) *The Encyclopedia of Edible Plants of North America*. New Canaan: Keats Pub.

Croke, A. (1830) *Regimen Sanitatis Salernitanum;a Poem on the Preservation of Health in Rhyming Latin Verse. Addressed by the School of Salerno to Robert of Normandy, Son of William the Conqueror, with an Ancient Translation:* Oxford,: D.A. Talboys.

Cruz, M. de la & Gates, W. (2000) Google-Books-ID: Dy0OUcmm-EhYC. *An Aztec Herbal: The Classic Codex of 1552*. Courier Corporation.

Culpeper, N. & Foster, S. (2019) *Culpeper's Complete Herbal*.

De Natale, A. & Pollio, A. (2012) A Forgotten Collection: The Libyan Ethnobotanical Exhibits (1912-14) by a. Trotter at the Museum O. Comes at the University Federico Ii in Naples, Italy. *Journal of Ethnobiology and Ethnomedicine*. [Online] 8 (1), 4.

Dogan, Y. (2012) Traditionally Used Wild Edible Greens in the Aegean Region of Turkey. *Acta Societatis Botanicorum Poloniae*. [Online] 81 (4), 329–342.

Duke, J. A. (1992) *CRC Handbook of Edible Weeds*. Boca Raton: CRC Press.

Duke, J. A. (1985) *CRC Handbook of Medicinal Herbs*. Boca Raton: CRC Press.

Ehrlich, G. & Hozeski, B. W. (2001) *Hildegard's Healing Plants: From Her Medieval Classic Physica*. Boston: Beacon Press.

Eland, S. C. & Lucas, G. (2013) *Plant Biographies*.

Elias, T. S. & Dykeman, P. A. (2009) *Edible Wild Plants: A North American Field Guide to Over 200 Natural Foods*. New York: Sterling.

Erasmus, D. (1878) *The Colloquies of Desiderius Erasmus Concerning Men, Manners and Things*. Vol. 2. Gibbings.

Eser, F. & Onal, A. (2015) Dyeing of Wool and Cotton with Extract of the Nettle (Urtica dioica L.) Leaves. *Journal of Natural Fibers*. [Online] 12 (3), 222–231.

Evelyn, J. (1699) *Acetaria: A Discourse of Sallets*. London: B. Tooke.

Facciola, S. (1998) *Cornucopia II: A Source Book of Edible Plants*. Vista: Kampong Publications.

Fernald, M. L. et al. (1996) *Edible Wild Plants of Eastern North America*. New York: Dover Publications.

Fiol, C. et al. (2016) Nettle Cheese: Using Nettle Leaves (Urtica dioica) to Coagulate Milk in the Fresh Cheese Making Process. *International Journal of Gastronomy and Food Science*. [Online] 419–24.

Folkard, R. (1884) *Plant Lore, Legends, and Lyrics*. London: Sampson Low, Marston, Searle, and Rivington.

Fox, F. M. et al. (1983) *Food from the Veld: Edible Wild Plants of Southern Africa Botanically Identified and Described*. Johannesburg: Delta Books.

Gardner, Z. E. et al. (eds.) (2013) *American Herbal Products Association's Botanical Safety Handbook*. Boca Raton: CRC Press.

Gerard, J. (1636) *The Herball or Generall Historie of Plantes*. London: Adam Islip, Ioice Norton, and Richard Whitakers.

Ghaima, K. K. et al. (2013) *Antibacterial and Antioxidant Activities of Ethyl Acetate Extract of Nettle (Urtica dioica) and Dandelion (Taraxacum officinale)*. 3 (5), 96.

Gibault, G. (1912a) *Histoire Des Légumes*. Librairie horticole.

Gibault, G. (1912b) *History of Vegetables*. Horticultural bookstore.

Grieve, M. M. (1998) *A Modern Herbal*. London: Tiger Books International.

Grigson, G. (1996) *The Englishman's Flora*. Oxford: Helicon.

Grzeszczuk, M. et al. (2016) Biological Value of Various Edible Flower Species. *Acta Scientiarum Polonorum Hortorum Cultus*. 15 (2), 109–119.

Guarrera, P. M. & Savo, V. (2016) Wild Food Plants Used in Traditional Vegetable Mixtures in Italy. *Journal of Ethnopharmacology*. [Online] 185202–234.

Guil-Guerrero, J. L. et al. (2003) Fatty Acids and Carotenoids from Stinging Nettle (Urtica dioica L.). *Journal of Food Composition and Analysis*. [Online] 16 (2), 111–119.

Guil-Guerrero, J. L. (2001) Nutritional Composition of Plantago Species (P. major L., P. lanceolata L., and P. media L.). *Ecology of Food and Nutrition*. [Online] 40 (5), 481–495.

Haines, A. (2010) *Ancestral Plants Volume 1: A Primitive Skills Guide to Important Edible, Medicinal, and Useful Plants*. Southwest Harbor: Anaskimin.

Hatfield, G. (2008) *Hatfield's Herbal: The Secret History of British Plants*. London: Penguin.

Henslow, G. (1905) *The Uses of British Plants Traced from Antiquity to the Present Day*. Ashford, Kent: L. Reeve & Co., Ltd.

Hryb, D. J. et al. (1995) The Effect of Extracts of the Roots of the Stinging Nettle (Urtica dioica) on the Interaction of Shbg with Its Receptor on Human Prostatic Membranes. *Planta Medica*. [Online] 61 (1), 31–32.

Hu, S. (2005) *Food Plants of China*. Hong Kong: Chinese University Press.

Hughes, R. E. et al. (1980) The Dietary Potential of the Common Nettle. *Journal of the Science of Food and Agriculture*. [Online] 31 (12), 1279–1286.

Irving, M. (2009) *The Forager Handbook: A Guide to the Edible Plants of Britain*. London: Ebury.

Jenner, T. (1653). *A Book of Fruits and Flowers*. The Rota.

Jman Redzic, S. (2006) Wild Edible Plants and Their Traditional Use in the Human Nutrition in Bosnia-Herzegovina. *Ecology of Food and Nutrition*. [Online] 45 (3), 189–232.

Kalia, A. et al. (2014) Pharmacognostical Review of Urtica dioica L. *International Journal of Green Pharmacy*. [Online] 8 (4), 201.

Kallas, J. (2010) *Edible Wild Plants: Wild Foods from Dirt to Plate*. Utah: Gibbs Smith.

Karalliedde, L. et al. (2008) *Traditional Herbal Medicines: A Guide to Their Safer Use*. London: Hammersmith.

Kavalali, G. M. (ed.) (2003) *Urtica: Therapeutic and Nutritional Aspects of Stinging Nettles*. Medicinal and aromatic plants--industrial profiles v. 37. London ; New York: Taylor & Francis.

Kays, S. J. (2011) *Cultivated Vegetables of the World: A Multilingual Onomasticon*. Wageningen: Wageningen Academic.

Kermath, BM et al. (2013) *Food Plants in the Americas: A Survey of the Domesticated, Cultivated, and Wild Plants Used for Human Food in North, Central and South America and the Caribbean*.

Kim, H. M. et al. (1998) Taraxacum officinale Restores Inhibition of Nitric Oxide Production by Cadmium in Mouse Peritoneal Macrophages. *Immunopharmacology and immunotoxicology*. 20 (2), 283–297.

King, J. & Felter, H. (1909) *King's American Dispensatory*. Ohio Valley Company.

Kress, H. (2018a) *Practical Herbs Vol. 1*.

Kress, H. (2018b) *Practical Herbs Vol. 2*. UK: Aeon Books.

Kuhnlein, H. V. & Turner, N. J. (1991) *Traditional Plant Foods of Canadian Indigenous Peoples: Nutrition, Botany, and Use*. Food and nutrition in history and anthropology v. 8. Philadelphia: Gordon and Breach.

Kunkel, G. (1984) *Plants for Human Consumption: An Annotated Checklist of the Edible Phanerogams and Ferns*. Koenigstein: Koeltz Scientific Books.

Lamb, P. (1710) Google-Books-ID: 4qeihp939xUC. *Royal Cookery; or, the Complete Court-Cook. Containing the Choicest Receipts in All the Particular Branches of Cookery, Now in Use in the Queen's Palaces, Etc.* Maurice Atkins.

Le Strange, R. (1977) *A History of Herbal Plants*. London: Angus and Robertson.

Lentini, F. & Venza, F. (2007) Wild Food Plants of Popular Use in Sicily. *Journal of Ethnobiology and Ethnomedicine*. [Online] 315.

Lim, T. K. (2012) *Edible Medicinal and Non-Medicinal Plants: Volume 1, Fruits.* Dordrecht: Springer.

Linnaeus, C. (1799). *Species Plantarum*. Impensis G. C. Nauk.

Loudon, J. C. (1835) *An Encyclopædia of Gardening: Comprising the Theory and Practice of Horticulture, Floriculture, Arboriculture and Landscape Gardening: Including All the Latest Improvements; a General History of Gardening in All Countries; and a Statistical View of Its Present State; with Suggestions for Its Future Progress, in the British Isles.* Vol. 2. Longman, Rees, Orme, Brown, Green, and Longman.

Łuczaj, Ł. (2010) Changes in the Utilization of Wild Green Vegetables in Poland Since the 19th Century: A Comparison of Four Ethnobotanical Surveys. *Journal of Ethnopharmacology*. [Online] 128 (2), 395–404.

Łuczaj, Ł. & Dolina, K. (2015) A Hundred Years of Change in Wild Vegetable Use in Southern Herzegovina. *Journal of Ethnopharmacology*. [Online] 166 297–304.

Luo, Z. H. (1993) The Use of Chinese Traditional Medicines to Improve Impaired Immune Functions in Scald Mice. *Zhonghua zheng xing shao shang wai ke za zhi = Zhonghua zheng xing shao shang waikf [i.e. waike] zazhi = Chinese journal of plastic surgery and burns*. 9 (1), 56–58, 80.

Mabey, R. & Blamey, M. (1974) *Food for Free*. London: Collins.

Mac Coitir, N. & Langrishe, G. (2015) *Ireland's Wild Plants: Myths, Legends and Folklore*.

Maggi, F. et al. (2012) A Forgotten Vegetable (Smyrnium olusatrum L., Apiaceae) as a Rich Source of Isofuranodiene. *Food Chemistry*. 135 (4), 2852–2862.

Maggi, F. et al. (2015) Essential Oil Chemotypification and Secretory Structures of the Neglected Vegetable Smyrnium olusatrum L. (apiaceae) Growing in Central Italy: Phytochemical Investigation of Smyrnium olusatrum. *Flavour and Fragrance Journal*. [Online] 30 (2), 139–159.

Manandhar, N. P. & Manandhar, S. (2002) *Plants and People of Nepal*. Portland: Timber Press.

Mascolo, N. et al. (1987) Biological Screening of Italian Medicinal Plants for Anti-Inflammatory Activity. *Phytotherapy Research*. [Online] 1 (1), 28–31.

Mawe, T. & Abercrombie, J. (1787) *Every Man His Own Gardener Being. Being a New, and Much More Complete Gardener's Kalendar and General Director, Than Any One Hitherto Published*. JF and C. Rivington, T. Longman, B. Law, J. Johnson, GGJ and J. Robinson, T. Cadell, W. Goldsmith, R. Baldwin, J. Murray, E. Newberry and W. Lowndes.

Menendez-Baceta, G. et al. (2012) Wild Edible Plants Traditionally Gathered in Gorbeialdea (biscay, Basque Country). *Genetic Resources and Crop Evolution*. [Online] 59 (7), 1329–1347.

Michael, P. & King, C. (2015) *Edible Wild Plants & Herbs: A Compendium of Recipes and Remedies*. Paperback edition. London: Grub Street.

Mills, S. Y. & Bone, K. (eds.) (2005) *The Essential Guide to Herbal Safety*. St. Louis: Elsevier Churchill Livingstone.

Mitich, L. W. (1988) Thistles Ii: Sonchus and Centaurea. *Weed Technology*. 2 (3), 380–381.

Morales, P. et al. (2014) Mediterranean Non-Cultivated Vegetables as Dietary Sources of Compounds with Antioxidant and Biological Activity. *LWT - Food Science and Technology*. [Online] 55 (1), 389–396.

National Institute of Science Communication (New Delhi, I. (2000) *The Useful Plants of India*. New Delhi: National Institute of Science Communication, Council of Scientific & Industrial Research.

Newall, C. A. et al. (1996) *Herbal Medicines: A Guide for Health-Care Professionals*. London: Pharmaceutical Press.

Nyerges, C. & Begley, E. (2014) *Guide to Wild Foods and Useful Plants*. Chicago Review Press.

O'Regan, P. (1997) Google-Books-ID: xaBRAgAACAAJ. *Healing Herbs in Ireland*. Primrose.

Paine, A. (2006) *The Healing Power of Celtic Plants: Their History, Their Use, and the Scientific Evidence That They Work*. Winchester: O Books.

Parkinson, J. et al. (1640) *Theatrum Botanicum: The Theatre of Plants; or, an Herball of a Large Extent*.

Pechey, J. (1707) *Compleat Herbal of Physical Plants*. H. Bonwicke.

Pechey, J. (1694) *The Compleat Herbal of Physical Plants; Containing All Such... Herbs, Shrubs and Trees, as Are Used in Physic and Surgery...; Also Directions for Making Compound-Waters, Syrups,... and Other Sorts of Medicines; More-Over the Gums, Balsams... and the Like... Sold by*

Apothecaries and Druggists; Are Added..., and Their Virtues and Uses... Described.

Pedersen, M. (2010) *Nutritional Herbology: A Reference Guide to Herbs*. Wursaw. Whitman Publications.

Pepys, S. (1887) *The Diary of Samuel Pepys. 1664-1665*. Cassell & Company.

Pieroni, A. (ed.) (2014) *Ethnobotany and Biocultural Diversities in the Balkans: Perspectives on Sustainable Rural Development and Reconciliation*. New York: Springer.

Pratt, A. (1856) *Common Thing on the Sea-Coasts. Sea Side Plants*. London: Society for Promoting Christian Knowledge.

Prendergast, H. D. V. & Sanderson, H. (2004a) *Britain's Wild Harvest*. Royal Botanic Gardens, Kew.

Prendergast, H. D. V. & Sanderson, H. (2004b) *Britain's Wild Harvest: The Commercial Uses of Wild Plants and Fungi*. Kew: Royal Botanic Gardens.

Pughe, J. (1861) *Meddygon Myddfai*. DJ Roderic; London, Longman & Company.

Quassinti, L. et al. (2014) Wild Celery (Smyrnium olusatrum L.) Oil and Isofuranodiene Induce Apoptosis in Human Colon Carcinoma Cells. *Fitoterapia*. [Online] 97133–141.

Quattrocchi, U. (2012) *CRC World Dictionary of Medicinal and Poisonous Plants: Common Names, Scientific Names, Eponyms, Synonyms, and Etymology (5 Volume Set)*. Boca Raton: CRC press.

Quinlan, F. J. B. (1883) Galium aparine as a Remedy for Chronic Ulcers. *British medical journal*. 1 (1172), 1173.

Râcz–Kotilla, E. et al. (1974) The Action of Taraxacum officinale Extracts on the Body Weight and Diuresis of Laboratory Animals. *Planta Medica*. [Online] 26 (7), 212–217.

Randall, R. E. (2003) Smyrnium olusatrum L. *Journal of Ecology*. 91 (2), 325–340.

Ray, J. (1724) *Synopsis Methodica Stirpium Britannicarum*. Innys.

Richardson, R. (1980) *Hedgerow Cookery*. Middlesex: Penguin.

Robinson, M. (1869) *The New Family Herbal: Comprising a Description, and the Medical Virtues of British and Foreign Plants, Founded on the Works of Eminent Modern English and American Writers on the Medical Properties of Herbs: To Which Is Added, the Botanic Family Physician; Valuable Medical Receipts; and Important Directions Regarding Diet, Clothing, Bathing, Air, Exercise, &c., &c.* William Nicholson.

Rohde, E. S. (1921) *A Garden of Herbs*. New York: Philip Lee Warner.

Ruel, J. (1522) *Pedanii Dioscoridis Anazarbei, De Medicinali Materia*. Lyon: Apud Balthazarem Arnolletum.

Runyon, L. (2007) *The Essential Wild Food Survival Guide*. Shiloh: Wild Food Company.

Rutto, L. K. et al. (2013) Mineral Properties and Dietary Value of Raw and Processed Stinging Nettle (Urtica dioica L.). *International Journal of Food Science*. [Online] 20131–9.

Said, A. et al. (2015) Highlights on Nutritional and Therapeutic Value of Stinging Nettle (Urtica dioica). *International Journal of Pharmacy and Pharmaceutical Sciences*. 7 (10), 8–14.

Salmon, W. (1710) *Botanologia: The English Herbal: Or, History of Plants*. Dawks, Rhodes and Taylor.

Salmon, W. (1693) *The Compleat English Physician*.

Samuelsen, A. B. (2000) The Traditional Uses, Chemical Constituents and Biological Activities of Plantago major L. a Review. *Journal of ethnopharmacology*. 71 (1–2), 1–21.

Sánchez-Mata, M. de C. & Tardío, J. (eds.) (2016) *Mediterranean Wild Edible Plants: Ethnobotany and Food Composition Tables*. [Online]. New York: Springer.

Silva, L. F. L. E. et al. (2018) Nutritional Evaluation of Non-Conventional Vegetables in Brazil. *Anais da Academia Brasileira de Ciências*. [Online] 90 (2), 1775–1787.

Simkova, K. & Polesny, Z. (2015) Ethnobotanical Review of Wild Edible Plants Used in the Czech Republic. *Journal of Applied Botany and Food Quality*. 88 (1), .

Small, E. (2006) *Culinary Herbs*. 2nd ed. Ottawa: NRC Research Press.

Storms, G. (1948) *Anglo-Saxon Magic*. [Online]. Dordrecht: Springer Netherlands.

Sturtevant, E. L. (1919) *Sturtevant's Notes on Edible Plants*. Albany: J. B. Lyon.

Tanaka, Y. & Nguyen, V. K. (2007) *Edible Wild Plants of Vietnam: The Bountiful Garden*. Bangkok: Orchid Press.

Thayer, S. (2006) *The Forager's Harvest: A Guide to Identifying, Harvesting, and Preparing Edible Wild Plants*. Ogema: Forager's Harvest.

Thornton, R. J. et al. (1814) *A Family Herbal: Or, Familiar Account of the Medical Properties of British and Foreign Plants, Also Their Uses in Dying, and the Various Arts, Arranged According to the Linnaean System*. London: B. and R. Crosby,.

Threlkeld, C. & Molyneux, T. (1727) *Synopsis Stirpium Hibernicarum Alphabetice Dispositarum. Sive Commentatio De Plantis Indigenis Presertim Dublinensibus Instituta. Being a Short Treatise of Native Plants, ... with Their Latin, English and Irish Names ... with an Appendix of Observations Made Upon Ol Plants. by Thomas Molyneux*. Powell.

Tokuda, H. et al. (1986) Inhibitory Effects of Ursolic and Oleanolic Ancid on Skin Tumor Promotion by 12-O-Tetradecanoylphorbol-13-Acetate. *Cancer Letters*. [Online] 33 (3), 279–285.

Topsell, E. (1658) *Historie of Foure-Footed Beasts; the History of Four-Footed Beasts and Serpents [microform]: Describing at Large Their True and Lively Figure, Their Several Names, Conditions, Kinds, Virtues (both Natural and Medicinal) Countries of Their Breed, Their Love and Hatred to Mankind, and the Wonderful Work of God in Their Creation, Preservation and Destruction: Interwoven with Curious Variety of Historical Narrations Out of Scriptures, Fathers, Philosophers, Physicians, and Poets*. G. Sawbridge, T. Williams, T. Johnson.

Topsell, E. et al. (1658) *The History of Four-Footed Beasts and Serpents*. London, Printed by E. Cotes, for G. Sawbridge [etc.].

Turner, N. J. et al. (2011) Edible and Tended Wild Plants, Traditional Ecological Knowledge and Agroecology. *Critical Reviews in Plant Sciences*. [Online] 30 (1–2), 198–225.

Turner, W. (1551) *A New Herball, Wherin Are Conteyned the Names of Herbes in Greke, Latin, Englysh, Duch, Frenche, and in the Potecaries and Herbaries Latin,: With the Properties Degrees, and Naturall Places of the Same*. London: Steven Myerdman.

Turner, W. & Britten, J. (n.d.) *The Names of Herbes, A.d. 1548. Edited, with an Introd., an Index of English Names, and an Indentification of the Plants Enumerated by Turner*. London: Published for the English Dialect Society by N. Trübner.

Uí Chonchubhair, M. (1995) *Flóra Chorca Dhuibhne: Aspects of the Flora of Corca Dhuibhne*. Baile an Fheirtéaraigh: Oidhreacht Chorca Dhuibhne.

Uphof, J. C. T. (1959) *Dictionary of Economic Plants*. New York: H.R. Engelmann.

Upton, R. (2013) Stinging Nettles Leaf (Urtica dioica L.): Extraordinary Vegetable Medicine. *Journal of Herbal Medicine*. [Online] 3 (1), 9–38.

Usher, G. (1974) *A Dictionary of Plants Used by Man*. London: Constable.

Valyova, M. et al. (2016) In Vitro Free-Radical Scavenging Activity of Aegopodium podagraria L. and Orlaya grandiflora (l.) Hoffm. (apiaceae).). *Journal of Chemical Technology and Metallurgy, 51(3)*. 51. 271-274.

Vehling, J. D. (1936) *Apicius, Cookery and Dining in Imperial Rome, a Bibliography, Critical Review and Translation of the Ancient Book Known as Apicius De Re Coquinaria*.

Vickery, R. (1997) *A Dictionary of Plant-Lore*. Oxford: Oxford University Press.

Vogel, G. (1977) 'Natural Substances with Effects on the Liver', in H. Wagner & P. Wolff (eds.) *New Natural Products and Plant Drugs with Pharmacological, Biological or Therapeutical Activity*. Proceedings in Life Sciences. [Online]. 1977 Berlin, Heidelberg: Springer. pp. 249–265.

Watson, R. R. (2018) *Dietary Interventions in Liver Disease: Foods, Nutrients and Dietary Supplements*. 1st edition. San Diego, CA: Elsevier.

Watts, D. (2007) *Dictionary of Plant Lore*. Amsterdam: Elsevier.

Wiersema, J. H. & Leon, B. (2013) *World Economic Plants: A Standard Reference*. Boca Raton: CRC Press.

Wyse Jackson, P. (2013) *Ireland's Generous Nature: The Past and Present Uses of Wild Plants in Ireland*. St. Louis: Missouri Botanical Garden Press.

Yunuskhodzhaeva, N. A. et al. (2014) Amino-Acid Composition of Urtica dioica Leaves and Polygonum hydropiper and P. aviculare Herbs. *Chemistry of Natural Compounds*. [Online] 50 (5), 970–971.

Zeipiṇa, S. et al. (2015) Antioxidant Activity in Nettle (Urtica dioica L.) and Garden Orache (Atriplex hortensis L.) Leaves During Vegetation Period. *Chemical Technology*. [Online] 66 (1), 29–33.

Zennie, T. M. & Ogzewalla, D. (1977) Ascorbic Acid and Vitamin a Content of Edible Wild Plants of Ohio and Kentucky. *Economic Botany*. 31 (1), 76–79.